WOMEN AND MONEY

WOMEN AND MONEY

Lorna Bourke

Thorsons
An Imprint of HarperCollins*Publishers*

Thorsons
An Imprint of HarperCollins*Publishers*
77-85 Fulham Palace Road,
Hammersmith, London W6 8JB

Published by Thorsons 1991

1 3 5 7 9 10 8 6 4 2

© Lorna Bourke 1991
Jacket design: Bev Speight

Lorna Bourke asserts the moral right to
be identified as the author of this work

A catalogue record for this book
is available from the British Library

ISBN 0 7225 2570 2

Typeset by Harper Phototypesetters Limited,
Northampton, England
Printed in Great Britain by
Woolnough Bookbinding Limited,
Irthlingborough, Northamptonshire

CONTENTS

$\mathscr{I}$NTRODUCTION

There have been enormous changes in the status of women in society in the past twenty years, in particular in their relationship with men, and in terms of work and earning power.

The advent of efficient contraception has meant that women can decide when they have children and can therefore plan their careers with greater certainty. A new generation of women is emerging – confident, self-possessed, increasingly with a career, and above all keen to make their own way in the world.

On the academic front, 44 per cent of all first class degrees awarded go to women and among newly qualified doctors and solicitors, 50 per cent are women. The number of women entering the accountancy profession has doubled this decade.

It may be difficult to believe, but women account for over 42 per cent of the country's workforce, filling some 12 million jobs – more than half of the total female population of 23 million.

Women dominate the employment scene in terms of numbers in many industries – retailing, advertising and the media and financial services such as banking and insurance. They are challenging men for the top jobs – and the top salaries that go with them.

Increasingly, the vast majority of married women own a share in the family home: in 1989, 67 per cent of home loans were granted to couples. The incidence of female ownership of homes is likely to continue to rise, as women tend to inherit from men.

For the average couple, buying for the first time, it would be impossible to get even a toe-hold on the home owning ladder without two incomes. Women's earnings are vital for any young couple if they are to be able to afford a home of their own. Even more importantly, women end up owning most of the money simply because they live longer than men. Over the next ten years, some £6.7 billion will be inherited in the UK and around half of it will be managed by women.

But the real revolution is in women's attitudes, particularly towards money. There is a fast-growing realization among women that managing their own financial affairs gives them much greater freedom; the advent of independent taxation for husbands and wives is hastening this development. Increasingly, women are not content to let men make all the decisions.

Are women's attitudes towards money different from their male counterparts'? For the working woman, probably not, and it will become less and less true of married women as they find themselves wrestling with the complexities of the tax system.

Although there are many areas where the solution to a financial problem is exactly the same for both sexes, there are some obvious situations where women's needs are clearly different from men's.

The vast majority of women marry and have children. Even if they return to work before the children are of school age, there may be a career break of several years.

As a result, women need to invest considerably more than men to provide themselves with adequate pensions. The lost years' National Insurance and pension contributions make a huge difference to the level of benefits. Couple this with the fact that women retire earlier and live longer than men and are therefore going to be much more vulnerable to the erosion of pension income through inflation, and it is obvious that women's pension needs are very different from men's.

Pensions experts have calculated that a woman of 25 will have to contribute 10 per cent more than a man to a pension scheme in order to buy the same yearly pension. If she takes a career break of five years to have a family, she will then need to contribute 50 per cent more to her pension scheme than a man.

Time was when marriage meant financial security and marrying well was socially important. With one in three of all marriages ending in divorce, women can no longer rely on a husband for support. Last year some 58,000 couples were divorced but the average divorced mother is obliged to work either full or part time to supplement any maintenance she may receive from her former husband. And of course, there are the men who simply refuse to pay, leaving the woman with major financial difficulties.

Recent legislation has not made things any easier for the divorced couple. In 1988 the rules were changed, making maintenance payments tax free in the hands of the wife, but abolishing all but the minimum of tax relief on maintenance payments for the husband.

In theory, this sounds fine; in practice, it has meant that for many middle-class couples, divorce is out of the question unless the wife has a career and is able to earn a significant amount.

What the new rules failed to take into account was that under the old system, maintenance payments from a former husband were, by judicious use of the children's personal tax allowances, tax free in the wife's hands anyway. Currently, the husband is not entitled to any significant tax relief on maintenance payments and as a result he can afford to pay even less.

Where the woman becomes the sole breadwinner through divorce, her financial needs are clearly very different from those of a married woman. Indeed, they bear closer resemblance to the financial needs of a man.

She loses all right to any widow's pension – either from the State or from her former husband's occupational scheme and she must ensure that provision is made on divorce to cover this loss of pension rights as well as insuring her ex-husband's life.

Yet it isn't just the increasing incidence of breakdown of marriage which is bringing about greater independence for women. Demographic changes mean that there will be a shortage of school leavers in the early 1990s. Employers will be looking to encourage married women to return to work to fill the employment gap. With the massive increase in computerization at all levels, it will be women with keyboard skills which can be upgraded who will be most in demand.

The Government has, belatedly, recognized the importance of women in the workforce and in the 1990 Budget introduced tax changes to encourage employers to set up workplace nurseries. The lack of adequate child care has been a major factor in many women's decision not to return to work, but in the coming decade, this will change as pressure from employers to extend child care tax incentives mounts.

What this means is that women increasingly have the financial muscle to be independent. A recent survey of women executives working for *The Times*'s top one thousand British companies, carried out on behalf of one of the major insurance companies, revealed that four out of ten high-flying women executives earn more than their husbands.

Women definitely want to be in charge of their own money and their destiny. This book shows you how to achieve this.

The chapters are divided into two sections: the first section highlights in general terms the different situations in which you are likely to find yourself. This paints a broad-brush picture of the problems you may encounter and their solutions.

The second section deals in detail with topics such as life assurance, pensions, savings and other specific areas of your finances. In these sections you should be able to find the answer to your particular situation.

Very few of us sit down and make a conscious effort to manage our money. What usually happens is that there is a change in our life – we get married, have a child, change jobs, buy a house – something which forces us to take a look at our finances. This book should help you to identify the situation and find the right solution for you.

WOMEN AND MONEY

Women have different financial needs from men for several reasons. Generally speaking, they marry and have children and there is usually a career break while the children are young. Also, women generally earn less than men, so they have less money to save.

Marriage is no longer the 'career for life' that it used to be and with one in three marriages ending in divorce, an increasing number of women find themselves in difficult financial circumstances, having to take on the responsibilities of the breadwinner. There are over a million single-parent families, the vast majority of which are headed by a single woman.

Women live longer than men, tend to inherit whatever assets have been acquired during the course of the marriage, and may find themselves late in life facing the situation of dealing with money for the first time.

It is better to learn to deal with your own financial affairs as the problems arise, rather than reach retirement and confront what might by that time be a very difficult or even insoluble situation.

The biggest single financial problem faced by most women has nothing to do with their sex; it is a problem shared by all low-paid workers.

But the situation is improving fast. Latest figures (April 1990) from the Department of Employment show average earnings for women full-time employees as £10,478 a year, and the figure is much higher in areas like London and the South East.

This has increased from £6,572 in 1985 and women's earnings are rising much faster than men's. In 1985, average earnings for a woman in full-time employment were 73.9 per cent of men's average earnings. By 1990, women's earnings had risen to 76.5 per cent of male average earnings, and that upward trend is continuing. Despite all these changes, women are still on average lower paid than men.

SINGLE WOMEN

With fewer responsibilities, the single woman has high spending power compared with her married counterpart, and is increasingly independent. Single women buy their own homes with their own earnings; they no longer wait to get married before making a purchase.

The Nationwide Building Society reveals that almost one-fifth of the society's homeowners are women – a figure which has more than doubled over the past 13 years. The vast majority of these women homebuyers are single – some 69 per cent of all female homeowners, compared with 34 per cent of men.

A higher proportion of Nationwide's first-time buyers were women. Some 48 per cent of women borrowers in England and Wales were buying for the first time, compared with 41 per cent of men.

Although most women still earn less than men, the Nationwide statistics confirm what we all know. Women are an economic force to be taken seriously. The statistics show that Nationwide's average woman borrower had an income of £12,704 a year in 1988 – a figure which had risen by 12 per cent since 1986.

Since then we have had wage inflation of around nine per cent a year, and the average woman borrower is now likely to be earning around £15,000 – probably as much as £20,000 a year in London and the South East.

All of which makes single women a tempting target for the life assurance salesman and others who sell financial products. Dealing with these people is important if you are to make the most of your money.

Bank accounts and borrowing

Over seventy per cent of the population have either a bank or building society account, or both. Most people open an account as a child or teenager and there are a host of savings accounts aimed specifically at this market. They are largely gimmicks and generally speaking, you will do better to go for the highest interest rate available. *Blay's MoneyMaster* in the reference section of your local library monitors all the accounts available and produces 'best buy' recommendations for various amounts of money invested over different periods.

Starting work or college is usually the trigger for opening a current bank or building society cheque account. There is little to choose between the major high street banks. All offer free banking if you keep your account in credit. Current accounts are often packaged with an automatic overdraft facility of around £2,000.

This is not necessarily the cheapest option, as the interest charged on these packaged facilities may well be higher than you could negotiate individually with your bank manager – although watch out for arrangement fees if you go the do-it-yourself route.

– Overdraft facilities

A good relationship with your bank manager is important, particularly if you need to borrow. So don't let your account run into the red without having arranged an overdraft facility. Unauthorised overdrafts carry penal interest rates of 30 per cent or more.

Of the big four high street banks, National Westminster probably has the edge on the others as it is the only bank of the four which is able to give independent financial advice. The other major banks are all 'tied' to their own in-house insurance or financial services company and can offer only the products of the company to which they are linked. The same applies to most of the major building societies. The Bradford & Bingley is the only one to offer independent advice. The table overleaf shows which bank or building society is tied to which financial institution and those that run a high interest cheque account.

If you are fortunate enough not to need an overdraft, you can open one of the bank or building society high interest cheque accounts which combine the convenience of a cheque account with interest paid on credit balances. Generally speaking, you will have to have a minimum of about £2,000 in the account to earn any worthwhile interest.

Credit cards and borrowing

Most banks will offer a credit card as soon as you open a current account; in many cases, even students are encouraged to take a credit card as a standard facility. Credit cards, and the newer debit cards like Switch and Connect are undoubtedly convenient. If you have difficulty controlling your finances, it is probably more sensible to go for a debit card rather than run up huge credit card debts that you may have difficulty repaying.

Bank and building society ties

Bank	Tie	High Interest Cheque Account	Minimum Investment
Barclays Bank	Barclays Life	✓	£1,000
Lloyds Bank	Black Horse Life and Pensions	✓	none
Midland Bank	Midland Life	✓	£2,000
NatWest	Independent	✓	£500
TSB	TSB Life	✓	£1
Abbey National	Friends Provident	✓	£1,000
Bradford & Bingley	Independent	✓	none
Halifax	Standard Life	✓	none
Nationwide Anglia	GRE	✓	£1
Alliance & Leicester	Scottish Amicable	✗	£1,000
Woolwich	Woolwich Life	✗	£1

Switch and Connect cards can be used in an increasing number of outlets. The cost of goods or services purchased with the card is debited to your bank account. If there is no money in the account or you have exceeded your overdraft limit, the transaction will be refused.

Credit cards like Access and Visa are equally convenient. You are given a credit limit and you can spend up to that limit, either settling the account in full or making use of the credit facility and paying off the balance over a number of months. Interest charges can be high – 28 per cent is not uncommon – and increasingly the credit card companies are making an annual charge for issuing the card.

Overdrafts at around five per cent over the bank base rate are cheaper than credit card borrowing, so it will generally pay to settle the credit card account in full each month, even if you have to increase your overdraft. Do check with the bank first and establish precisely what rate you are being charged on the overdraft.

Charge cards like American Express and Diners Club do not offer a credit facility and your account must be settled in full at the end of each month. Gold cards, first introduced by American Express, have, among other facilities, an automatic overdraft – usually £10,000 – at a preferential rate and this is probably the cheapest way of borrowing.

But you will need an income of around £25,000 a year to be eligible.

Store cards issued by the big retailers may be either credit cards or charge cards, although the former is more common.

Generally, you are better off avoiding store cards altogether. With the exception of the credit card issued by the John Lewis Partnership, the interest charged on store account cards is higher – sometimes much higher – than that charged on credit cards. Interest charges of 32 per cent or more are not uncommon.

However, in the case of Marks and Spencer, which will not accept anything but its own credit card, you have no choice.

Personal loans

The high street banks and building societies will generally offer you a personal loan if you want to borrow money for any length of time. These are packaged and are designed to cope with borrowing for larger purchases such as a new car or music system rather than tiding you over a difficult financial patch.

The range of the packaged loans is from one to five years and for sums of £500 to £5,000. Larger loans will probably have to be separately negotiated.

In the case of the building societies, some have packaged unsecured personal loans but more often they would suggest a further advance, secured on your property.

Personal loans are not the cheapest way of borrowing – you will generally pay around 21 per cent for a packaged loan, compared with three to seven per cent over the bank base rate for an overdraft.

With a personal loan, the total interest is added at the beginning of the period and you make monthly repayments based on the amount borrowed, plus the interest for the period, divided by the number of months, or the term, of the loan.

Overdrafts are, however, cheaper at around three per cent to seven per cent over the bank base rate and you can negotiate the terms individually with your bank manager. An overdraft can be paid off as and when you have agreed to do so. This may be in regular instalments, variable instalments or simply when you know you will receive a lump sum from, say, an inheritance, or the maturity of a savings plan.

Loan accounts which operate like an overdraft, where interest is charged only on the outstanding balance, are the cheapest method of borrowing, but it may be difficult to persuade your bank manager to give you one.

Work and pensions

One of the first major financial decisions to be made is likely to crop up when you start work. Most large firms have occupational pension schemes and you will have to decide whether or not to join. The decision will depend largely on the strength of the company scheme – but as a general rule it will pay to belong to one. Most company schemes include a contribution from the employer – often, it is quite generous. With a personal pension plan, you have to make the contributions yourself, usually without any help from your employer.

– 'Final salary' pension schemes

Company pension schemes come in two types – 'final salary' schemes and 'money purchase'. A final salary scheme is one where the benefits are linked to your earnings at retirement age.

In a good scheme, you would get one-sixtieth of your final salary for every year of service with the company. After forty years of service, you would retire on the maximum permitted, which is currently two-thirds of your final salary.

Almost without exception, you will find that companies with final salary schemes make a contribution to the pension fund – in many cases, this can be as much as 15 per cent or more of the payroll. With the best schemes, the employee makes no contribution at all.

For this reason, it is generally worth joining an occupational scheme if it is linked to your final salary. Two contributions are bound to be better than only one; you will have a proportion of your salary deducted at source which goes into the pension fund, and the employer will make contributions too.

The attraction of final salary schemes is that if the money in the fund when you reach retirement is not sufficient to pay the promised benefits, it is your employer who has to foot the bill – not you.

– 'Money purchase' pension schemes

With a money purchase occupational pension scheme, you get the benefits you pay for – and your employer must also make a contribution. The value of the pension at retirement will depend entirely upon how much has been contributed and how well the money has been invested.

The pension paid at retirement may bear no relationship to the salary you are earning at retirement. It will only be worthwhile joining a money purchase scheme if your employer makes a reasonable contribution.

If it is simply a group money purchase scheme to which your employer makes little or no contribution, you will probably be better off taking out a personal pension, which will be less trouble when you change jobs.

Anyone joining a pension scheme now must by law have any benefits earned preserved until retirement age, so you won't lose out by joining one. In many cases, you will be able to transfer those benefits to a new company scheme when you change jobs, or take them into a personal pension.

In the past, the contributions of employees who changed jobs and left company pension schemes – 'early leavers', as they were called – were used to subsidise the pensions of those who stayed with the firm until retirement age. This is no longer the case. (See Chapter 3 on page 68 for more details on pensions, including personal pensions.)

If the company you work for does not have a pension scheme, do not automatically rush out and buy a personal pension. While it is undoubtedly true that the earlier you start to make provision for your retirement, the more you are likely to receive later, bear in mind that money invested in a pension scheme cannot be returned to you, except at retirement age; even then, only a proportion of it can be taken as a cash lump sum.

Savings

Sit down and work out what you want to do with your cash. However little you earn, it is always a good idea to get into the habit of saving regularly.

Make a budget and decide how much you are obliged to spend on general overheads – rent, gas, electricity, telephone, travelling, car costs, insurance, holidays, clothes and miscellaneous expenditure. Then set aside a sum to save.

How you save will depend on your objectives. If it is for short-term needs like holidays or Christmas presents or an emergency fund, you will almost certainly be best off putting it in a high interest bank or building society account.

Charges are low, and your money is instantly accessible. You will probably need to open one anyway so that your employer can pay your salary direct into a bank account. The table on page 14 shows which major banks and building societies offer high interest cheque accounts.

You may be able to obtain a better rate of interest from the small building societies but you will invariably have to deal with the account by post, which may not always be convenient. The Saturday finance pages of the quality newspapers regularly carry features on the best rates available, or you can check in your public library which should have a copy of *Blay's MoneyMaster*, a monthly publication which monitors all the accounts on offer and identifies the 'best buys' at various levels of saving. Chapter 2 on page 39 gives full details.

Longer-term saving is different and you must decide on your objectives and the length of time over which you are prepared to commit your cash.

If you don't own your own home, the chances are that you will be saving up to buy a place of your own. Although 100 per cent loans are now freely available to first-time buyers, you will still need cash for legal and surveyors' fees, stamp duty at one per cent of the purchase price if the purchase price is over £30,000, not to mention carpets, curtains and furniture.

Money being saved to buy a home is not money with which you can afford to take risks, nor do you want to have it tied up in insurance-linked long term savings contracts with hefty penalties for withdrawal before maturity. Put it in the bank or building society and to stop yourself from spending it on other things, opt for a three or six months notice account.

This will not be a handicap if the money is used to buy a house or flat because it will take at least three months to find somewhere suitable, make an offer and get to the point of having to stump up the cash. (See Chapter 4 on page 94 on buying a house.)

Regrettably, many young people are sold life assurance-linked savings schemes which are not suitable for their needs. These are only suitable if you have a known longer-term need. A good deal of life assurance is sold by persuading you to save through a savings-type with profits, or unit linked endowment policy.

Life assurance is about providing financially for disaster, whether through death, sickness or accident. Saving, which is what with profits and unit linked endowment contracts really are, is another matter entirely and a life policy is often not the best vehicle for your savings because of the high penalties for surrender in the early years. (Full details on savings appear in Chapter 2, page 39.)

Life assurance

If you are single, there is only one type of life policy which you really need – convertible term insurance.

It is very cheap, and will pay out a lump sum of money if you die before an agreed date. It also carries the option to convert into other types of policy at a later date without you having to give any evidence of good health.

Many life companies will not offer life assurance to women who have been treated for pre-cancerous conditions following a smear test, for example. Convertible term insurance – preferably with the right to increase the sum assured during the agreed term – insures your right to get life cover. This will be especially important if you get married and have children.

Convertible term cover is cheap. For example, a 26-year-old woman would pay approximately £10 a month for convertible term cover, which would provide £100,000 if she died within twenty years of taking out the policy.

But even this type of cover is optional if you need every penny you earn to put towards buying a place of your own. Remember, if you have no dependants you don't need life assurance of any sort.

Even mortgage protection, a policy which pays out a sum sufficient to pay off your mortgage if you should die before the home loan matures, is not essential unless you have dependants.

Do bear in mind, however, that elderly parents could become dependants, in which case it could be worthwhile converting your convertible term policy to whole life – the sort that pays out a lump sum, whenever you die.

It will also be worthwhile considering Permanent Health Insurance, particularly if you are self-employed. This pays a weekly sum if you are unable to work through accident or sickness.

The types of policy that everyone will be keen to sell you are the savings type with profits and unit linked endowments. The difficulty with these (even if you want to save long term) is that initial charges are high and they are very inflexible – your money is tied up. If you want to cash in before the policy matures, you will probably get a very poor deal, particularly in the early years of the policy.

When you come to buy a house, a with profits endowment or a pension policy may be the right way to invest long term to pay off the loan. But until then you would probably be better off saving elsewhere. Full details of the different types of life assurance are in Chapter 5, page 120.

Long term saving

Once you have your own home, you will eventually have to make another decision. Do you intend to stay single, or are you hoping to marry – because this will affect how you manage your money long term.

Many women will at some stage have a child or children. It is likely that the time will come when you will want to have access to your savings, either to subsidise the household income when you give up work to have children or for other expenditure on items such as school fees, holidays and the like.

If you put all of your money into a pension scheme, you will not be able to get any of it back until retirement age. If you expect to remain single, you can afford to put significant sums of money into a pension scheme – either a company fund or a personal pension – and should consider doing so. You will have no pension from a husband to rely upon, but neither will you be obliged to give up work and use your savings, unless you decide to have children without being married.

Remember that the sooner you start to save for retirement, the less you will need to invest to provide a realistic level of income. See Chapter 3, page 68 for full details on pensions.

It is never wise, however, to put all your eggs in one basket, so even if you pay significant sums into a pension scheme, it would be sensible to have other types of savings such as Tessas (Tax Exempt Special Savings Accounts) and PEPs (Personal Equity Plans).

In terms of flexibility and low charges, there is virtually nothing to beat a unit or investment trust regular savings scheme. Additionally, if it is held within a Personal Equity Plan, you pay no income tax on the dividends, nor is there any liability to capital gains tax when the shares or unit trusts are sold.

Charges on PEPs are low and they are very flexible – you can cash in without penalty at any time. But because the value of the underlying investments – the unit, investment trusts, or shares – are linked to the fortunes of the stockmarket, you really ought to be able to take a five-year view at least, otherwise you may well find that share prices have collapsed, as they did in October 1987, just when you need your money. Equity-based investments should only be considered once you have accumulated a nest egg in ready cash in the bank or building society. Turn to Chapter 2, page 39 for full details on the different types of savings opportunities.

In later life, many single women find themselves looking after elderly relatives. If you are an only child, this is something you must consider and take into account when you are saving.

There are home annuity schemes which would provide extra cash to help care for an elderly relative, but the elderly person must be a homeowner and over 70 before they are viable.

LIVING TOGETHER

Women who cohabit have particular problems in a number of financial areas, the most important of which is property. If you own a property in your sole name, your partner could still be entitled to a share in it if he or she has paid part of the mortgage.

Conversely, if the property is in your partner's name but you pay household bills, buy food, and share the running expenses of the car, you will be on extremely shaky ground if you try to claim a share of the property. If the property is owned by you both as joint tenants, you will almost certainly be entitled to a half share and will automatically inherit the whole property on the death of your partner. But if it is owned as tenants in common, it may be owned in varying proportions set out in the deeds – and on death, your share or your partner's share could be left to someone else.

As a joint tenant you will be jointly and severally liable for the mortgage payments, so if your partner is unable to pay his or her share, you will be liable for the full monthly repayment.

The abolition of multiple mortgage interest relief in August 1988 has meant that there is no longer any advantage in remaining unmarried so far as buying property is concerned.

When renting property, it is safer to have the lease or agreement in both names. You will both be individually liable for the whole of the rent, but the landlord cannot object to you sharing the property.

Contents insurance presents another problem. Unless both names are on the policy, the insurance company might treat your partner as a 'visitor', in which case his or her belongings may well not be covered.

Life assurance

Like any married couple, you may want to insure both your life and your partner's life to provide for each other if you die. You can do this in a variety of ways, the easiest of which is by naming each other as the person entitled to the benefit, writing the policies in trust naming each other as the beneficiaries, or each assigning the benefits of the policy to your partner.

If you are cohabiting, this may affect eligibility and entitlement to some Social Security payments.

Taxation

When tax relief was obtainable on maintenance payments, there used to be a tax advantage in living together rather than marrying. Where there was one or more children, one partner could sue the other for maintenance and the payer was entitled to tax relief on these payments. Where there were two incomes and two or more children, both partners could sue each other for maintenance and both obtain tax relief on the payments. It was not unheard of for couples in this situation to totally wipe out their tax liability. This is no longer possible, and most of the tax advantages of living together as opposed to marrying have now disappeared.

Making a will

Women who cohabit generally have no fixed rights to the partner's property, except where it is owned jointly, unless assets are specifically bequeathed in a will.

If you are cohabiting with someone and they die intestate, you are entitled to nothing although you can make a claim on the estate if you can show that you were supported by your partner – particularly where there are young children.

If you live with a married man who is separated from his wife, any will he has made in her favour will still be valid.

These are just a few of the important points to bear in mind when living together.

MARRIAGE AND MOTHERHOOD

It is precisely because most women do get married and have children that their financial needs are so different from men's.

As a married woman or an unmarried mother you will probably have career breaks when children come along and you cannot therefore expect to contribute as much as a man to a pension. On the other hand, if you are married, you are entitled to a widow's pension should your husband die either while working or in retirement – something a single woman cannot rely upon.

Tax

This is not meant to be a comprehensive guide to taxation – there isn't room in a book of this kind to go into details. But the tax situation concerning married women has changed for the better. Before April 1990, the first financial decision a woman had to make on marriage was whether to opt for separate taxation or separate assessment or be taxed jointly with her husband.

With the introduction of independent taxation in April 1990, this is no longer a problem. No decision has to be taken – you will automatically be taxed independently. Similarly, the married man's allowance has been replaced by a married couple's allowance, which goes to the husband in addition to his own personal allowance. If his income is insufficient to take full advantage of this allowance, any excess goes to you as his wife.

This means that you have your own personal allowance which can be offset against your income, whether it is earned or investment income. Prior to April 1990, a wife's investment income was always treated as though it were the income of the husband and taxed accordingly, at his top rate of tax. The wife with investment income only could not offset her personal allowance against her investment income.

If you are a non-working wife and you and your husband have savings, it will now pay to transfer into your name sufficient assets to take advantage of your personal allowance which could not be used in the past. For example, in 1991-92 the personal allowance is £3,295 if you are under 65, £4,020 if you are over 65 and £4,180 if you are over 75. Assuming your savings are earning 10 per cent before tax, you can transfer up to £32,950 into your name before you become liable to tax on this income.

Bear in mind that if you have income from employment, self-employment or a pension, this has to be taken into account.

If you have a joint bank or building society savings account, the Inland Revenue will deem that the income from that account is shared equally, unless you specifically state otherwise. Most joint accounts have tax deducted at source because the husband is usually a taxpayer. If you opt for separate accounts, a non-taxpaying wife can receive interest gross, without deduction of tax, by filling in a simple declaration when the account is opened. With a joint account, the non-taxpaying wife usually has to reclaim the tax deducted at source.

Independent taxation also means that wives have their own capital gains tax allowance. The first £5,500 of profits made in the current tax year on investments such as shares, unit or investment trusts, or property are completely free from CGT. Profits above this level are taxed at your income tax rate although you cannot use your personal allowances against capital gains.

Single women and women cohabiting with a partner are not affected by independent taxation.

Budgeting

Once the honeymoon is over – and some advisers might suggest before you get married – it would be sensible to sit down and go over your joint finances. The same applies to couples living together. More problems are caused in relationships over money than almost anything else.

Even if you are both responsible about money, you will save yourself a lot of arguments if you work out what your overheads are on rent or mortgage repayments and household bills and open a joint account out of which the bills are paid. You may want to contribute an equal amount to the joint account on a monthly basis. Alternatively, you may decide to pay in an amount in proportion to your relative earnings.

For example, supposing the household bills amount to £650 and you take home £165 net a week while your husband takes home £210. You could pay in £286 a month to the joint account to cover bills and your husband £364 – in proportion to your take-home pay. A joint account is always useful. In the event of the death of a spouse, the remaining partner is able to obtain access to funds in a joint account. If the deceased partner has everything in his or her own name, the survivor cannot touch it until after probate or letters of administration have been granted.

Buying a house
Buying a house together is likely to be the next financial event that will require decision-making. Having dealt with the practicalities of which type of loan to take (see Chapter 4, page 94 for full details), you will have to decide whether to own the house as joint tenants or as tenants in common.

Most married couples decide to be joint tenants. This means that should one partner die, the other automatically inherits the other's share. This may not be suitable, however, if one or both partners have been married before and there are children from the previous marriages.

In this situation, you may want to be tenants in common, which means that each partner can leave his or her share of the house to the children – or to whoever else he or she wishes to benefit.

Making a will
At this point, it is sensible to consider making a will, particularly if one or both of you have assets in addition to the family home. Do not put it off, thinking that it is only important once you get older. If you die without making a will, whatever your age, your partner will not automatically inherit everything – even if you are married.

The table overleaf shows who receives what under the laws of intestacy.

Who gets what if you die intestate

Beneficiaries	Net Value of Estate		
	Up to £75,000	£75,000 to £125,000	£125,000 plus
Spouse with children	Everything	£75,000+ [1]	£75,000+ [1]
Spouse without children	Everything	Everything	£125,000+ [2]
Children	Equal Shares*	Equal Shares of half remaining estate	—
Others**	—	—	half remaining estate

* *Only if there is no surviving spouse.*
** *Other beneficiaries in order of priority are parents of the deceased, brothers and sisters of the deceased, children of the siblings.*
[1] *All personal chattels plus a life interest in half the remaining estate. This reverts to the children on the death of the second partner.*
[2] *All personal chattels plus a life interest in half the remaining estate.*

Inheritance tax planning

Making a will is vital for married couples in avoiding or minimizing any liability to inheritance tax. This tax is payable on death on the value of your estate above a certain threshold. For 1991-92, the starting point for inheritance tax is £140,000. Any assets in excess of this figure will be taxed at 40 per cent.

At this level, many people will have an inheritance tax liability through owning their own home.

You can avoid inheritance tax by giving your assets away to your children (or anyone else) and there is no tax liability, provided you live for at least another seven years.

Clearly, if both partners to a marriage can leave £140,000 before inheritance tax becomes payable, it will pay to split the assets between the two partners where there are assets in excess of this figure, or assets which are likely to be worth more than this.

Transfers between husband and wife are free from any tax liability, either during their lifetime or upon death. If the assets are held largely in one partner's name, they will be free of inheritance tax upon death, when they will pass to the surviving spouse. But on the death of the second partner, only the first £140,000 will be free of inheritance tax. If both partners have assets, the first £140,000 from each estate can be left tax-free to the children or to anyone else without incurring a tax charge.

Since women live longer than men, married women tend to inherit the family assets. Frequently, the major asset is the family house and this can pose an inheritance tax problem. If you give the house to the children but continue to live in it, this does not avoid inheritance tax. It is deemed by the Inland Revenue to be a gift with reservation and inheritance tax will still be payable when you die. The only way to avoid inheritance tax in this situation is to give the house to the children and pay them a realistic rent which you may well not be able to afford.

Where assets have been given away, it is clearly sensible for either you, or the recipient, to insure your life for a term of seven years to cover the period when there will be a tax charge – albeit diminishing – if you die. The table below shows the tax liability if you die within seven years of giving assets away.

Death in Years	Rate of Inheritance Tax
1 to 3	40%
4	32%
5	24%
6	16%
7	8%

If you are unable or unwilling to give assets away, for example where your home is your main asset, you can cover the liability which will occur when you die by taking out whole life assurance. This will pay a sum of money sufficient to cover the tax liability when you die. The younger you are when you take this out, the cheaper it is. See page 125, Chapter 5 for fuller details of whole life assurance.

Inheritance tax planning is a complicated area and it will pay to take specialist advice from a tax lawyer, accountant or independent financial adviser.

Children

Until children come along, you will probably not need to revise your finances too much. But as soon as the first one is on the way, if not before, there are a number of areas for consideration. If you have been earning, you will need to work out how you will manage to pay the mortgage or rent, and other household outgoings with only one salary if you are giving up work. This will vary, depending on your individual circumstances. Lone parents have the toughest time of all, and most are largely dependent on Social Security payments of some sort or another.

You may intend to return to work fairly rapidly after the baby is born, but be prepared to change your mind. Many women find that once the baby arrives, contrary to their expectations, they would prefer to stay at home and look after it themselves.

You may be entitled to maternity leave and maternity pay from your employer. This will be taxable in the normal way, but State maternity benefits are tax free. To qualify for Statutory Maternity Pay (SMP), you must have been employed by the same employer without a break for at least six months prior to the 26th week of pregnancy, and your average gross weekly earnings must have been £52 a week or more for the 1991-92 tax year.

You will be entitled to SMP for eighteen weeks and it is paid for the first six weeks at the rate of 90 per cent of your basic weekly salary, provided you have worked for the same employer for sixteen hours a week or more for at least two years, or, if you have worked part-time, between eight and sixteen hours a week for at least five years. For the remaining twelve weeks, SMP is paid at the flat rate of £44.50 per week.

If you have been working for the same employer for at least six months, but less than two years, you will be paid £44.50 per week for eighteen weeks.

To get the full eighteen weeks' SMP in either case, you must have stopped working by the beginning of the sixth week before the expected date of confinement. Some women may elect to work an extra couple of weeks or more beyond that date; if you do decide to continue working, it is likely that you may forfeit part of your SMP entitlement for that six-week period, but will be compensated by being paid your full salary as long as you are working.

The self-employed or others who do not qualify for Statutory Maternity Pay may be able to claim Maternity Allowance, which is also a flat rate of £40.60 a week, plus £24.50 a week for each dependant, paid for eighteen weeks. Your local Social Security office will be able to give you full details of these and other Social Security benefits to which you may be entitled.

If you intend to return to work, find out as early as possible if your employer runs a workplace crèche or nursery (an increasing number do since tax concessions were introduced in the 1990 Budget) or find out about the costs of au pairs, nannies, local childminders or nurseries. The latter usually have long waiting lists. Official childminders have to be registered with your Local Authority.

Once the baby is born, you will be entitled to tax-free Child Benefit of £9.25 a week (from October 1991) for a first child, £7.50 for subsequent children. Single parents are eligible for an extra benefit of £5.60 a week. None of these payments are related to your income.

You should also consider what would happen if you were to die and leave your husband or partner with a young child or children to bring up. A recent survey by a major insurance company revealed that dealing with the children was the biggest single concern of men faced with the prospect of losing a wife.

One in three men questioned admitted that they would have difficulty looking after the children, rising to one in five among men with young children, and nearly half thought they would have to leave work if their wife died.

It clearly is not just your husband's life which should be insured, but yours as well. The insurance company calculated that the value of a wife's work, if she had to be replaced by paid helpers, would be at least £370 a week.

The best way of covering this risk, if you haven't already insured yourself, is with convertible term assurance which will provide a lump sum, should you die within the agreed term of the policy. See Chapter 5, page 120 for full details.

The term of the policy needs to be sufficiently long – say fifteen years – to cover you for the period when the children are growing up and still at school and it should have the option to increase both the benefits and the premiums to take account of inflation.

If as a family you are dependent on your earnings to pay for the basics such as the mortgage, you should also consider taking out Permanent Health Insurance (PHI). This provides a monthly income if you are sick and unable to work.

Even if you do not work, consider what would happen if you were seriously ill and unable to look after the children. Permanent Health Insurance is limited for the non-working wife and not all insurance companies offer this facility.

Permanent Health Insurance replaces your income – usually up to a maximum of 75 per cent of your earnings – and provides cash to cover your share of the family outgoings.

In the case of a non-working wife, it will provide a sum of money – albeit generally restricted to a maximum of around £75 a week – which will go some way towards paying for help in the home. See page 130, Chapter 5, for details.

School fees

Once the first child is on the way, you will have to decide whether you are prepared to have your children educated in the State system or privately. Be realistic about this. The current cost of sending a child to Eton, for example, is over £3,500 a term without extras and even a middle-ranking, fee-paying school will work out at around £2,500 to £3,000 a term. Fees for a day pupil at a prep-school will be around £1,200 a term.

Remember, even if you think you can afford it today, circumstances may change and to remove a child from a fee-paying school halfway through his or her studies can be damaging.

If you decide to send your children to fee-paying schools, the sooner you make financial provision for this, the better. Like all forms of investment, the longer your money has to accumulate in a school fees plan, the better the return will be.

It may be that grandparents or godparents are prepared to help out with a lump sum or you might be saving from income. Either way, you will need specialist advice.

Whoever you consult, remember that all school fees plans are about savings or investment and there is nothing special about being linked to a life assurance policy, as so many schemes are. In the end, it is how your investments perform that really matters. Because of the high penalties for encashment in the early years, life assurance-linked school fees plans are not generally suitable unless at least ten years pass before fees become payable. The same is true of most equity-linked investments – those invested in shares, unit or investment trusts.

For shorter-term saving – whether it is for school fees or anything else – opt for the security of fixed interest investments.

Do bear in mind also that the cost of education does not stop when the children leave school. Higher education at university, college or polytechnic can be every bit as expensive as sending children to fee-paying schools. Grants for further education have now been replaced with loans for students, so you have the option of subsidizing your offsprings' university careers or allowing them to get into debt. If you decide to subsidize a child's higher education, it is unlikely to cost less than £3,000 a year.

School fees planning is a specialist area and one where it will pay to take independent advice.

Children's savings

The investment decisions you will face won't just be about investing your own money. Once children come along, grandparents and other friends and relatives will inevitably give the children money and you must decide what to do with this.

Remember, if you or your husband give the children money or investments, any income above £100 from those investments will be treated as though it belonged to the giver and taxed accordingly. Each child has his or her own personal tax allowance – £3,295 for 1991-92 – and can have income up to this amount before becoming liable to tax.

Most children are non-taxpayers, so if you are looking for security, choose an investment account with a bank or building society. Interest can be paid without deduction of tax on completion of a simple form when the account is opened for the child. National Savings Bank's Investment Account pays interest without deduction of tax auto-matically but you do have to give one month's notice of withdrawal, so if the child wants to operate the account, this may not be convenient.

If the money is to be put away for, say, seven years or more, you can consider the whole spectrum of equity investments. Chapter 2 on Savings gives full details of the options.

Returning to work

While the children are young, you may want to stay at home with them. If you have no earnings you will not be able to contribute to a pension scheme. Even significant savings are no help in this context because you are only entitled to tax relief on pension contributions on earnings.

Any pension benefits earned from former employment or self-employment will be frozen within the scheme or personal pension and you will be able to take them at retirement.

If you return to work at a later date you will be better off contributing to your own pension scheme – whether through your employer's scheme or through a personal pension – rather than your husband paying extra on his contributions.

This is because statistically, your husband is likely to die before you and the widow's pension which you would receive is generally paid at half the rate of the full pension, whereas any pension you earn in your own right will be paid in full throughout your lifetime.

Of course, if you can afford to do both, it will pay to do so. (See Chapter 3, page 68 for full details on pensions).

DIVORCE

With one in three marriages ending in divorce, you have to be realistic about the likelihood of this happening. In terms of finances, there is little you can do to prepare for this unless you have significant assets of your own. But if you are concerned about your future finances, keep any assets which you own prior to the marriage in your own name. There has been a recent move to legalize pre-nuptial agreements, but they have never been tested in the courts. It is impossible to insure against divorce.

Recent legislation has encouraged divorcing couples to go for the 'clean break' – a once and for all financial settlement – particularly where there are no children.

The court will be concerned to see that the children are properly provided for, but do not automatically assume that you will be allowed to stay in the family home. As a general rule of thumb, on divorce where there are children involved, you might be entitled to half the assets of the marriage, plus a third of the joint incomes.

Where the wife is the higher earner, this could be too onerous on the husband and the court will take this into account when approving a settlement.

Even in a simple, straightforward break-up where you part amicably, you will need to consult a solicitor. The Solicitor's Family Law Association will be able to recommend a solicitor in your area who specializes in divorce.

Many are prepared to give preliminary advice for a fixed fee and you may be entitled to legal aid. Legal aid is means tested and the qualifying thresholds are very low, so if you have any significant earnings or savings, you are unlikely to qualify.

It is difficult to generalize about finances on divorce – much will depend on individual circumstances. Unless the break-up is amicable, your most immediate problem is likely to be how the bills are paid. If you have no money coming in, notify your mortgage lender at once and ask for a payment holiday until such time as a settlement is reached.

Go to your local Social Security office and find out what State benefits you may be entitled to. Close any joint account at the bank or building society if you think your husband may take all the cash.

If the separation is amicable, you will presumably have come to a temporary arrangement over money until you get to court and any maintenance settlement is finalized.

Income tax and maintenance
The rules on the taxation of maintenance payments were changed in March 1988. Since then, any maintenance payments made to you by your former husband under agreements made since that date will be tax free in your hands.

Once divorced, you will be entitled to the usual personal tax allowance to offset against your income. If there is a child or children, you will also be entitled to the Additional Personal Allowance, which brings the personal tax allowance up to the level to which a married man is entitled – though you may have to split this with your former husband, depending on your relative contributions towards the children's maintenance.

However, your former husband's ability to be generous over maintenance has been seriously restricted, since he now receives only minimal tax relief on maintenance payments. Prior to 1988, he was entitled to full tax relief on all payments made.

Before 1988, maintenance payments were taxable in the wife's hands. But by splitting the maintenance and paying some direct to the children (each of whom is entitled to their own tax allowance) and some to the wife, it was possible for most divorced mothers to avoid paying any tax at all. The situation now, although simpler, is not so advantageous for the majority of ex-wives in receipt of maintenance payments, as most husbands are no longer entitled to tax relief on maintenance payments, and will therefore pay less.

There are some important points to bear in mind before you agree a divorce settlement. Firstly, you will no longer be entitled to any benefits from your former husband's occupational or personal pension plan either on retirement or death, unless he makes specific provision for this. Even if he does, his second wife will have a prior claim if he remarries and has more children. Secondly, you lose your entitlement to a State widow's pension on the death of your former husband.

If you work, you will have to pay full National Insurance contributions once you are divorced. Up to the time of the divorce you will be entitled to a State pension when you retire, based on your former husband's contributions.

If you are negotiating maintenance payments, you must ensure that the sum includes sufficient for you to pay the premiums on a term assurance policy on his life. When he dies, your maintenance dies with him and you need to protect yourself during the time the children are growing up.

You should also review your own life assurance arrangements. As a single woman, all your life policies should be written in trust for the benefit of your children, to avoid them being included in your estate and subject to Inheritance Tax.

Also bear in mind that your maintenance payments cease if you remarry, although payments to the children will continue.

If you are capable of earning a worthwhile sum yourself, or you are seriously considering remarriage in the near future, it might pay to opt for no maintenance for yourself and settle for a larger proportion of the assets.

Divorce cancels any will you or your former husband have made, so you should both make a new one. If he remarries and changes his will, leaving everything to his second wife and children, you may have a claim on the estate if he has been supporting you and your children.

His new wife may be a wealthy woman or be a high earner. Some judges may be persuaded to take this into account when assessing how much your husband can afford to pay in maintenance, others ignore it. And, of course, she is not obliged to reveal anything, so proving that she is wealthy is frequently impossible. In any event, no judge would expect her to finance payments made to you.

Finally, be realistic. If one income is now supporting two families, there is no possibility of your being able to live as well as when you were married. Do not pursue your former husband for money at the expense of the children's happiness – however vindictive you may feel. If you were not working before the divorce, being obliged to work may not be easy at first – but it might prove to be the beginning of a satisfying career.

WIDOWHOOD

Once you have been widowed you are presented with a financial situation which is largely immutable. It is best to consider widowhood as a possibility while your husband is still alive. Find out what life assurance he has and what he may be entitled to from his employer. (It is usually three to four times gross earnings.) If it is not sufficient, ensure that he increases it – or if you can afford it, volunteer to pay the premiums yourself.

Make sure you know whether you will be entitled to a widow's pension from his employer's scheme and how much it is likely to be in relation to your current income. If he is self-employed or not a member of a company scheme, ask what personal pensions he has and to what you might be entitled.

Persuade your husband to make a will, because if he dies intestate, you will not necessarily inherit all his assets (see page 26 for details).

These are gloomy questions to ask, but if you don't you could find yourself in desperate straits as a widow. State benefits are so low that you will have difficulty surviving. And if you know what provision has been made for you and the children, it will help in planning your own affairs.

Above all, if you have earnings of your own, and you are not a member of an occupational pension scheme, consider taking out a personal pension yourself. This is more efficient in any case than relying on the widow's benefits from your husband's personal pension. (See Chapter 3 on Pensions for full details.)

Make sure you have at least one joint bank or savings account to ensure that you will have access to cash in the event of your husband's death. His personal accounts will all be frozen until Probate is granted.

As a widow you will be entitled to a special tax allowance, Widow's Bereavement Allowance, which is equal to the difference between the married and single personal allowances. This can be offset against any widow's pension you receive or any other income from, for example, investments. It is not a Social Security payment. You can claim this for the tax year in which your husband dies and for the following year, unless you remarry.

The emotional problems of widowhood are likely to be overwhelming initially and you are unlikely to be in a sensible frame of mind to deal with any long-term financial arrangements. Beware of the unscrupulous financial adviser who offers to deal with everything. Do not tie up any money you have, or may inherit, for long periods of time yet.

Contact your local Social Security office and establish the State benefits to which you may be entitled, such as Widowed Mother's Allowance. You are eligible for this if you have a child or children for which you are entitled to claim Child Benefit. Widowed Mother's Allowance is currently £52 a week plus £10.70 a week for each child.

You may also be able to claim the State widow's pension, currently £52 a week, if you are 45 or over when your husband died, provided he made enough National Insurance contributions. If he had not, you will still be entitled to a non-contributory Widow's Benefit of £31.25 a week.

Assuming your husband has made some financial provision, you will probably have the proceeds of one or more life policies and death benefits from a former employer to invest. Make sure you take independent advice and check that the adviser is a member of one of the Self Regulatory Organisations, such as FIMBRA or IMRO, listed at the end of Chapter 6.

SINGLE PARENTHOOD

There are over a million single parents in this country, the vast majority of them divorced or unmarried mothers. Many of the problems which confront widowed or divorced women apply also to single parents. How you cope with being a lone parent will depend very much on whether you deliberately chose to be an unmarried mother and whether the father is happy to support you, both financially and emotionally.

The vast majority of single parents qualify for Social Security benefits, with a high proportion totally dependent on them. The table below shows the main benefits to which you might be entitled.

State Benefits – weekly rates – 1991-92

Income Support - Means Tested	
Single Parent - under 18	£23.65
special rate - under 18	£31.15
18 and over	£39.65
dependent children under 11	£13.60
aged 11 to 15	£20.00
aged 16 to 17	£23.90
aged 18	£31.40
Lone Parent Premium	£4.45
Child Benefit - Non Means Tested	
First child	£9.25
Other children	£7.50
One Parent Benefit	£5.60
Housing Benefit - Means Tested	
This will depend on the amount of rent	
paid and your other income.	

The rules on eligibility are complicated, particularly if you are cohabiting, and the means tested benefits will be affected by income from earnings, maintenance payments and investments. The amount of capital you have will also affect both your eligibility and the amount of the benefit.

Visit your local Social Security office to establish your benefit entitlement. The National Council for One Parent Families and your local Citizens Advice Bureau can help if you feel you are not being given a benefit to which you are entitled. Both have long experience of dealing with Social Security claims and the legal problems of single parenthood, divorce, custody and maintenance.

If you have given up work to have a child, you will probably also be eligible for National Insurance credits under the home responsibilities scheme. (This also applies to divorced mothers, widowed mothers, or anyone looking after an elderly relative.) This is important, as it will affect the amount of State retirement pension to which you are entitled. Leaflet NP27, Looking After Someone At Home, gives details; these are available from your local Social Services department or office.

Lone parents who have been abandoned by their partner may find pressure applied by the local Social Security office to disclose the whereabouts of the partner in order to qualify for Social Security payments. If you are not prepared to do so, contact The National Council for One Parent Families for advice; see page 156 for their address and telephone number.

$\mathscr{S}$AVINGS AND INVESTMENT

Women do have different investment needs from men, not least of all because they tend to outlive their spouses or partners. This has two effects: they may inherit whatever assets there are, and frequently find themselves late in life having to deal with money for the first time.

Secondly, if they are widowed, they may find themselves trying to run a household on a reduced income. A widow's pension, whether from the State or from an occupational scheme, is never as much as the full pension paid while their partner is alive.

With an increasing proportion of women working, women should make their own pension provision rather than relying on benefits from their partners' or spouses' schemes.

Nowadays, one in three marriages end in divorce and increasingly the courts are encouraging couples to settle for a 'clean break', leaving the woman with a lump sum to provide both a new home and income.

But a woman's attitude towards money often differs from the male approach. No statistical research exists to prove it, but men are generally greater risk takers than women. This can make a profound difference when considering an investment, as the degree of risk involved in a particular form of investment is in direct proportion to the potential returns.

Women's investment needs are very similar to men's, until they make a decision to have children, whether or not they are married. The differences stem from the career break or the end to paid employment which most mothers experience. This affects the length of time when women have money to save or to contribute to a pension scheme.

Whatever your situation, it is important to analyse your finances and make sensible provision for the future.

Chapter 1 on page 11 deals specifically with the financial issues connected with divorce, parenthood, widowhood and retirement.

SAVINGS AND INVESTMENT

Savings and investment are very similar – with savings, you are putting away regular sums of money on a weekly or monthly basis. Investment is generally understood to mean a lump sum.

Savings and investment fall into two distinct categories: low risk interest-bearing investments and higher risk equity-linked schemes investing in shares. Your choice will depend very much on the purpose of your saving or investment and the degree of risk with which you feel comfortable. It is no use putting your money into shares if the fact that they could fall in value gives you sleepless nights.

The point to bear in mind at all times is that the actual or potential return on any investment is in direct proportion to the risk. Nothing ventured – nothing gained. Even with fixed interest type securities, such as an income bond, there is still a risk. If you are receiving nine per cent after tax on, say, a guaranteed income bond, but inflation is running at 11 per cent, you are eating into your capital at a rate of two per cent a year. A balanced approach, spreading your assets across a wide range of both fixed interest and equity-based investments, is the best policy.

While it doesn't require a great deal of expertise to shop around and uncover the best deal on a bank or building society savings account, or the cheapest interest rate on a credit card, there is no doubt that any equity-linked investment is a very different kettle of fish.

If you want to make the most of your savings, you will need good, impartial advice from an independent financial adviser when it comes to choosing the right unit or investment trust, with profits endowment policy, or spread of shares.

Planning your savings and investments

Most people start saving in a haphazard fashion. You open a bank account when you start work and when you discover that you are not spending all your monthly earnings, you open either a building society account, or transfer some of the surplus to a high interest account at the bank.

This is fine, but it is much better to sit down and analyse your saving and investment needs and objectives. If you are the sort of person who always spends as much, or more, than you earn, getting into the savings habit at an early stage will stop you squandering your money.

The type of investment vehicle you choose will depend on a number of factors:

– *Whether you are saving short term or longer term*

If you are likely to need your money within five years, say as the deposit on a home of your own, or for a round-the-world trip, then equity-based investments like shares, unit or investment trusts and equity-based life assurance products such as with profits endowments are not really suitable.

Although it is possible to make considerable profits short term in, for example, shares, equity-based investments, because of their volatility, should really be viewed as longer term investments with a minimum five year commitment. Life assurance-based savings should definitely be viewed as long term commitments. The surrender penalties make these very poor value for money if they are cashed in within five years and you must be prepared to take a ten year view at least.

– *Are you investing for income or capital growth?*

Retirement, widowhood, divorce and motherhood are the four main areas where women are likely to find themselves investing for income. If you are dependent on income from investments to maintain your living standards, then you can probably afford to take fewer risks. But even if you are risk averse, you must make some provision for inflation if both your capital and income are not to diminish in real terms and your spending power be eroded.

If you are widowed relatively early in life and are largely or totally dependent on investing the proceeds of your husband's life policy to provide income, you cannot afford to ignore the long term effects of inflation.

– *How much risk can you afford to take without worrying?*

Long term, there is no doubt that the returns from shares and collective investments like unit and investment trusts have outstripped an investment in a bank or building society account. The table overleaf

Value of £1,000 invested over varying periods to 1.8.91

Years	Building Society Account	Average UK Growth (Unit Trust)	Average UK Growth (Investment Trust)	FTA All Share Index
	£	£	£	£
3	1,281.61	1,161.78	1,025.62	1,423.01
5	1,462.20	1,613.57	1,385.61	1,881.60
7	1,721.58	3,033.36	2,577.74	3,250.68
10	2,185.07	4,688.40	3,886.56	5,392.90
15	3,296.52	11,947.85	17,681.13	13,898.20

Unit and investment trust returns are calculated on an offer to offer basis with net income reinvested.
Source: Micropal

illustrates this point. But if you are going to have sleepless nights worrying about your investments, think again.

What are you saving or investing for?

– Under one year
Holidays, Christmas, birthdays, a large item of household equipment (eg fridge, microwave) known expenditure on predictable events (eg medical fees for a minor operation, or new school uniforms when the children change schools).

Suitable investments – bank or building society high interest or notice accounts, gross interest onshore or offshore bank or building society accounts, (for non-taxpayers) National Savings Investment Account.

– One to five years
Deposit on a first home, a new car, major items of household expenditure (redecoration, new kitchen or bathroom, loft extension, swimming pool, conservatory).

Suitable investments – bank and building society Tax Exempt Special Savings Accounts (Tessas) (taxpayers only), gross interest onshore or offshore bank or building society accounts (for non-taxpayers), bank or building society high interest or notice accounts, National Savings Investment Accounts, National Savings Certificates, National Savings Capital Bonds, National Savings Yearly Plans, short-dated gilts (Government stocks), income bonds, deferred annuities.

With any of the above investments, the precise vehicle you choose or mix of investments will depend on the relative returns at the time. For example, the National Savings Investment Account, paying 10.25 per cent without deduction of tax, equivalent to 7.68 per cent to a basic rate taxpayer, shows a poor return compared with a building society high interest account from which it is possible to obtain a return of 8.25 per cent, basic rate tax paid.

The same is true in the one- to five-year category where the highest returns are obtainable from Tessas, paying anything up to 11 per cent tax free. This is well above the return on National Savings Certificates, which pay 8.5 per cent tax free. The difference is that the return on most Tessas fluctuates, whereas the payout on the 36th Issue of National Savings Certificates is guaranteed.

Over the coming five years, only time will reveal which is the better investment. National Savings might increase its interest rates to become competitive at a time when variable interest rates are falling.

The conclusion must be that you have to keep abreast of what is on offer. Today's 'best buy' might look pretty uncompetitive two years down the line. Moreover, even within the same savings institution you cannot guarantee that you will be informed of better investments.

A common grouse among bank and building society investors is that they put money into an account because at the time it is being promoted, the interest rate is attractive, only to find a year or so later that the institution has launched a better account – but has not told existing investors.

– Five to ten years or more
Saving or investing for school fees and higher education, retirement, long term career change involving a drop in earnings, care of an elderly relative, paying off a mortgage, or loan to start a business.

Suitable investments – for savings over five years, virtually the whole investment spectrum opens up, ranging from shares, commodities, futures and options, unit and investment trusts as well as fixed interest investments as mentioned for shorter term savings.

The only exceptions are life assurance savings contracts such as with profit endowments and unit linked policies. These have to run for ten years or more to be 'qualifying' contracts and there are potential tax pitfalls for higher rate taxpayers if you cash in or make them paid-up within ten years (seven years if it is a ten-year endowment).

In addition surrender penalties and charges are high in the early years so you must be certain that you can keep the policy in force for at least ten years before this type of investment is worthwhile.

TAXPAYER OR NON-TAXPAYER?

The investments you choose will depend to some extent on whether or not you are a taxpayer. This is less of a consideration with many equity-based investments like shares or unit trusts where, with the exception of income funds, the dividend income is so low as to be negligible. With this type of investment you are looking for capital growth.

Non-taxpayers

There are an estimated 14 million non-taxpayers in the UK – largely children, non-working wives, pensioners and other people on very low incomes. There are only two interest-bearing investments which cater specifically for non-taxpayers – National Savings Investment Account and bank and building society gross accounts, onshore and offshore. All pay interest gross without deduction of tax.

However, it is only since April 1991 that banks, building societies and other deposit-taking institutions have been allowed to pay interest gross to non-taxpayers. Up until then, non-taxpayers had tax deducted at source from all bank and building society investments, and this tax was not reclaimable.

With the advent of independent taxation, the old composite rate tax system was abandoned and now all non-taxpayers can receive their interest gross provided they complete a simple declaration that they are a non-taxpayer when they open the account.

Now that there is tougher competition for non-taxpayers' savings, National Savings may improve its rate on its Investment Account. Keep an eye on the comparative rates.

Do not be seduced into investing in a Tessa (Tax Exempt Special Savings Account). As a non-taxpayer, a tax free investment has few charms and you will get a better return, with fewer restrictions, from an onshore or offshore deposit account.

Gross accounts are likely to continue to show a better return than even tax free investments. To find out which bank or building society is offering the best return, you should consult *Blay's MoneyMaster*, which you will find in the reference section of your public library. This is a monthly publication which monitors all the bank and building society accounts on offer – instant access, monthly income, notice accounts – and comes up with 'best buys' in each category. A subscription to *MoneyMaster* costs £98 a year, but is only worth considering if you have very large sums of money to invest.

Taxpayers

In recent years, the Government has been doing away with tax relief on most forms of saving, so with one or two exceptions, the investment vehicle you choose will depend entirely on what you want from your investment as the return is generally taxable.

Tax relief on life assurance savings scheme premiums was abolished in the 1984 Budget, so only policies taken out before that date will have this tax advantage. Payments from long term life assurance savings schemes are generally still tax free after ten years. See Chapter 5 for details.

However, while the Government was busy removing tax concessions from life assurance savings schemes, it was creating tax benefits on three other forms of investment – PEPs (Personal Equity Plans), Tessas (Tax Exempt Special Savings Accounts) and BES Schemes (Business Expansion Schemes).

Because of the tax breaks on these investments, they should be a part of all taxpayers' portfolio. And, of course, if you are a higher rate taxpayer, the benefits are that much greater.

Both PEPs and Tessas allow you to take income, tax free. In addition, equity investments held within a PEP are free from capital gains tax

(CGT), the tax charged on all profits realized above £5,500 a year (1991-92). This threshold is generally increased each year in line with inflation.

Investments in a BES scheme qualify for tax relief on up to £40,000 worth of investment a year and the profits are free from CGT after five years. Full details of PEPs, Tessas and BES schemes appear on pages 56, 48 and 66.

National Savings Certificates offer a tax free return over the five year period. The 36th Issue shows a return of 8.5 per cent and is attractive to anyone paying tax at 40 per cent.

Basic rate taxpayers may be able to get a better return from a Guaranteed Income Bond or from a bank or building society account.

FIXED RATE INVESTMENTS

Generally speaking, you can make a decision about most interest bearing investments yourself, simply by comparing terms and conditions and shopping around. The Saturday finance pages of the quality newspapers regularly publish tables of bank and building society 'best buys' on investment accounts as well as the latest National Savings Rates and Guaranteed Income Bond returns. Alternatively, you can consult *Blay's MoneyMaster*, which monitors the various rates paid on all interest bearing investments, except gilts.

Bank and building society accounts

The banks and building societies offer a wide range of investment accounts with varying terms and conditions. Generally speaking, the longer you are prepared to commit your savings, the higher the return. But with fierce competition for savers' money, there can be wide variations in the rate of return paid on very similar accounts.

It definitely pays to shop around and to keep an eye on the competition, because the society offering the best return now may not be the best buy six months or a year down the line.

Most bank and building society accounts offer a variable rate of interest; very few pay a fixed rate. Some building societies occasionally offer a guaranteed fixed return, generally over fairly short periods like one year. But these are limited offers and you have to move fast if you want to invest.

The high street banks offer seven day, one month, three months and sometimes six month notice accounts which pay fixed rates. Clearly, if you think interest rates are falling, it will pay to choose a fixed interest account; when they are rising, go for the variable return.

Building societies, and to a lesser extent the high street banks, offer a range of accounts. Most popular are the instant access accounts with no penalties for withdrawal. Some of the best returns are offered by the smaller societies, which have fewer branches, and you may have to conduct the account by post. If you want easy access and perhaps a cash card or cheque book, go for one of the top ten societies with plenty of branches.

Top ten building societies

Name of Society	Cash Card	Cheque Book	Monthly Income Account	1 Month Notice Account	3 Months Notice Account
Halifax	✓	✓	✓	✗	✓
Nationwide	✓	✓	✓	✗	✓
Woolwich	✓	✓	✓	✗	✗
Alliance & Leicester	✓	*	✓	✗	✓
Leeds Permanent	✓	✗	✓	✗	✓
National & Provincial	✓	✗	✓	✗	✓
Cheltenham & Gloucester	✗	✗	✓	✗	✗
Bradford & Bingley	✓	✗	✓	✓	✓
Britannia	✓	✓	✓	✗	✗
Bristol & West	✓	✓	✓	✓	✗

NB: Abbey National is now a bank   * Through Girobank

Tax

Bank and building society interest has basic rate tax deducted at source unless you are a non-taxpayer in which case you can receive the interest gross, without deduction of tax, provided you sign the requisite declaration.

Higher rate taxpayers will have a further 15 per cent tax liability on all interest received. If you have £50,000 or more to invest, the high street banks will pay you the interest gross, without deduction of tax, regardless of whether you are a taxpayer or not, but the interest is taxable.

Tessas

Tessas, Tax Exempt Special Savings Accounts, were introduced in the 1990 Budget and have been available since January 1991. They are an investment which all taxpayers should consider, provided they can afford to have their money tied up for five years. Non-taxpayers will do better elsewhere.

Tessas are bank or building society accounts on which the interest earned is tax free as long as you leave the original capital invested untouched for five years.

The interest earned can be left to roll up tax free or taken as income, in which case it is paid net of basic rate tax. For example, if you had earned £400 in interest during the course of the year on your Tessa, you would be allowed to withdraw £300. The £100 tax retained remains within the Tessa and is paid out at the end of the five years, provided you have left the capital untouched. If you withdraw any of the capital, you lose the tax concessions.

Anyone aged 18 or over can take out a Tessa and you can invest a maximum of £9,000 over five years – £3,000 in the first year and up to £1,800 in years two to five. You are allowed only one Tessa but you can switch it from one bank or building society to another. Beware of switching penalties imposed by some building societies and banks and bear in mind that many Tessas have loyalty bonuses paid after five years which you will lose if you move.

Most Tessas pay a variable rate of interest, a few offer a fixed return – some just for the first year, occasionally for the full five years.

You get the best return if you invest the maximum lump sum at the beginning of each year, but you can save up to £150 a month provided the bank or building society offers this facility. Not all of them do.

National Savings

National Savings offers a variety of interest-bearing investments which can be bought over the Post Office counter. The terms and conditions vary but to obtain the maximum, you must generally hold the investment for the full term. Early encashment will involve penalties. It is important to bear this in mind when investing, because National Savings interest rates do not change as frequently as interest rates on competing bank and building society accounts. While this is an advantage when interest rates are coming down, you could end up out of pocket over a period of prolonged interest rate rises.

National Savings Investment Account

This account pays interest gross without deduction of tax, and is therefore suitable for non-taxpayers. Gross interest is paid automatically and you do not have to make a declaration that you are a non-taxpayer, but the interest is taxable. The current rate is 10.25 per cent paid without deduction of tax, equivalent to 7.6 per cent to a basic rate taxpayer.

However, you have to give one month's notice of withdrawal. Children, one of the biggest groups of non-taxpayers, might find this difficult to understand. Interest is variable, but the rate paid is not always competitive with other gross paying accounts on offer from the banks and building societies. The minimum investment is £5, the maximum is £25,000.

National Savings Certificates

These are five-year investment certificates paying a guaranteed tax free return at the end of the period. The return is usually pitched at a level to make Savings Certificates attractive to higher rate taxpayers. The 36th Issue offers a return of 8.5 per cent tax free. A higher rate taxpayer would have to earn over 14 per cent gross on investments to equal the tax free return on the 36th Issue. Basic rate taxpayers can generally get a better return with fewer restrictions from a building society account.

You can invest up to £5,000 in the current issue and up to £10,000 in addition if you are reinvesting the proceeds of earlier issues which have now reached maturity. National Savings Certificates should always be encashed or reinvested on maturity, as the rate of interest paid on mature issues is only 5.01 per cent.

Savings Certificates can be purchased in units of £25. You can withdraw your money before the five year term is up but the rate of return will be less. You do not, however, lose the tax benefit. No interest is earned on certificates repaid in the first year.

You can also invest up to £5,000 in 5th Issue Index Linked National Savings Certificates, which offer a return in line with increases in the Retail Prices Index plus a bonus of 4.5 per cent a year. This is obviously most attractive at a time when inflation is expected to rise.

Yearly Plan is aimed at regular savers who do not have a lump sum to invest in Savings Certificates. You save between £20 and £200 on a monthly basis for a year to buy a Savings Certificate which you must then hold for a further four years to earn the maximum guaranteed return over the five year period of 8.5 per cent tax free.

Higher rate taxpayers who benefit the most from the tax free return on Savings Certificates are unlikely to need to save regularly and there are more attractive alternatives to Yearly Plan (such as Tessas) for basic rate taxpayers.

Childrens' Bonds

National Savings has introduced a Children's Bond, a five year investment paying a return of 11.84 per cent tax free. At the time of writing, this is a competitive rate even compared with gross paying bank and building society accounts, but whether it will remain so is another matter.

The structure of the bond makes it relatively unattractive. If you cash in before the five year term is completed, the return is only five per cent a year – there is a massive loyalty bonus at the end which brings the return up to 11.84 per cent. About the most attractive feature of it is the certainty and the fact that parents and other relatives can invest on behalf of the child without any tax problems. The maximum investment per child is £1,000; the minimum is £25.

National Savings Income Bonds

These are aimed at elderly people who need monthly interest to supplement their income. The rate of interest paid (currently 11 per cent) is variable, but is paid gross, without deduction of tax, every month. It is, however, taxable if you are a taxpayer. The rate of interest paid is displayed in Post Offices and six weeks' notice of any change in the rate is given. However, you have to give three months' notice of withdrawal and during times when interest rates are rising fast, you could find yourself locked in and unable to earn a better return.

Minimum investment is £2,000 and bonds can be added to in multiples of £1,000 up to the maximum of £25,000. The bonds are ten-year investments and if encashed within the first year, only half the published interest rate is paid.

Generally speaking, building society monthly income accounts offer higher returns, and are more flexible with shorter notice periods for withdrawal. Most societies offer both gross interest (for a non-taxpayer) or net interest on a monthly income account.

National Savings Capital Bonds

These are aimed at investors who want a guaranteed return but do not need income – probably someone just a few years off retirement who does not want to run the risk of holding shares or other equity-based investments because of the possibility of a collapse in the stock market.

The bonds pay a guaranteed return which is fixed for five years. Interest is paid gross and added to the original investment. At the time of writing, a £100 initial investment is guaranteed to be repaid at £172.34 at the end of the five-year term – a return of 11.5 per cent gross over the period.

Capital Bonds generally do not offer such good returns as Guaranteed Growth Bonds sold by life assurance companies, and are less flexible in that you have no choice on the term – only five years. Insurance companies sell guaranteed growth bonds for varying terms of one to five years. The return is taxable.

Minimum investment in Capital Bonds is £100 with a maximum of £100,000. You can cash in your bonds at any time by giving three months' notice, but if you cash in before the end of the five years the return will be lower.

Premium Bonds

These are not investments but a straightforward lottery. Buy these for fun. Prizes range from £250,000 to £50, tax free. Anyone aged 16 or over can buy Premium Bonds or parents, grandparents or guardians can buy them for a child. The minimum value that you can buy is £100 for the over 16s, £10 if the bond is bought for a child; the maximum holding is £10,000. Bonds are not entered into the draw until they have been held for three months. They can be sold back at any time for the original amount.

National Savings Ordinary Account

This account is now so uncompetitive in terms of the rate of interest paid that it is not worth bothering about. The banks and building societies offer more attractive instant access accounts. About the only thing to recommend the Ordinary Account is that the first £70 of interest paid in any year is tax free. However, even this does not compensate for the poor rate of return.

Save As You Earn

This regular savings plan is only available to employees who are entitled to buy shares in their company under an approved Share Option Scheme. Ask your employer for details.

Gilts – Government stocks

Government stocks, or gilts as they are known, are IOUs issued by the Government. They are suitable investments for anyone who needs a guaranteed return over a fixed period of time.

They have many uses in areas such as school fees planning and providing income during retirement. For example, on retirement you may decide to put, say, two-thirds of your money into long dated gilts paying 10 per cent. If you hold them until they mature, your income will remain constant. The other third might be put into an equity-based investment like unit or investment trusts to provide some capital growth which would offset the effects of inflation on your static income from the gilts.

Parents wanting to provide school fees at some time in the future might decide to buy a portfolio of 'low coupon' gilts maturing in successive years. These offer very little income because the 'coupon' or interest paid is low. But they are generally bought at a large discount to the nominal or face value and have a built in tax free capital gain if held to maturity.

You might pay only £86 for every £100 of stock maturing in, say, 1998. This gives you a guaranteed capital gain – tax free – of £14, provided you hold the stock until it is redeemed in 1998.

A parent or grandparent might decide to invest a lump sum in six gilts maturing in successive years to pay all or part of a child's school fees. This has the advantage of certainty.

How do gilts work?

Gilts offer a fixed rate of return over a fixed period with the guarantee of your money back at the end of the term. The Government issues them, pitching the interest rate in line with current interest rates available on similar investments elsewhere.

However, because gilts can be traded on the Stock Exchange, the price of a gilt if you buy or sell before the gilt matures will fluctuate to reflect current interest rates. If a gilt was issued with a 'coupon' or interest rate of say, 10.5 per cent and current rates are only eight per cent, the price of the gilt will rise. Had rates risen to 13 per cent, the price of the gilt would have fallen.

In other words, you can only be certain of the return you will get on a gilt if you are prepared to hold it to maturity. If you sell before then, the price you get may be more or less than you paid.

Gilts bought at a discount to their face value – say £88 for every £100 of stock – have a guaranteed tax free capital gain if you hold them to maturity. Gilts bought at a premium to their face value – say, £111 for every £100 of stock – have a guaranteed capital loss if you hold them to maturity.

For the novice investor wanting to lock into a known interest rate for a fixed period of time, gilts are the only way of doing so for periods longer than five years. Under five years, and you will find it simpler to buy guaranteed income bonds or growth bonds from a life company.

Do not invest in gilt unit trusts. The charges are ridiculously high and you would be better off investing direct through the Post Office or buying through your bank or stockbroker.

– Buying and selling gilts

Gilts on the National Savings Stock Register can be bought over the counter at the Post Office. The advantage of this is that the interest payments, or dividends, which are made half yearly, are paid gross, without deduction of tax. This is useful for non-taxpayers. The dividends are, however, taxable, although any profits made on selling or redemption are not subject to capital gains tax.

If you buy through your bank or stockbroker, dividends will be paid net of basic rate tax and non-taxpayers will have to reclaim the tax deducted at source.

The disadvantage of buying or selling gilts through the Post Office is that you do not know the price at which you have bought or sold them, as the transaction is carried out by post. When interest rates are moving fast, this is a very real disadvantage since you do not know what the yield, or return, will be.

For example, Treasury 9.5 per cent 1999 is selling at £98 and is showing a yield to redemption of 9.93 per cent. The yield to redemption is made up of the £2 guaranteed capital gain which you will make when the stock matures in 1999 plus the annual interest payments at 9.5 per cent. You pay £98 for every £100 of stock which will be redeemed in 1999. If the price moves to £99 there is only £1 of capital gain and the yield to redemption falls to just over nine per cent.

If you buy or sell through your bank or stockbroker, you can get a price and yield that day and buy or sell immediately. However, a stockbroker will make a minimum commission charge of around £20. The cost of buying £1,000 worth of gilts through National Savings is £4.

Unless you are sure you know precisely what you want to buy and for what purpose, it will pay to take independent advice.

Guaranteed Income and Growth Bonds

Like gilts, guaranteed income and growth bonds (not to be confused with National Savings Income Bonds) are used to provide a guaranteed return over a fixed period of time – very useful for someone dependent on investment income for their day-to-day needs.

Your original investment is repaid in full at the end of the agreed period. Income bonds also provide a guaranteed fixed income over the period. Growth bonds allow the interest to roll up and interest is repaid at the end of the term with the original investment.

Guaranteed income and growth bonds are issued by life companies and the proceeds are free from basic rate tax. Higher rate taxpayers may have a further 15 per cent liability. They are generally available in terms from one to five years. Income bonds are bought mainly by elderly people wanting a guaranteed supplement to their pension in retirement. Occasionally, the income may be used to fund the annual payments on a life policy of some sort or meet school fees or other known expenditure where one cannot afford to take risks.

Growth bonds are more often bought by investors in the run-up to retirement, when they are still working and do not need the income. A growth bond has none of the risks of equity-based investments and provides a guaranteed sum at retirement. They are, like gilts, also used in some school fees planning.

EQUITY INVESTMENTS

The underlying securities in all equity-based investments, whether they are unit or investment trusts, savings type life policies or PEPs (Personal Equity Plans), are shares in companies. The returns from shares are not guaranteed.

As the name implies, you own a share of the business and if the company fails, you may lose all of your money. On the other hand, if the business goes well, the price of your shares will rise to reflect this fact.

Any form of equity investment is inherently more risky than an interest-bearing deposit like a bank or building society account, but the potential rewards are much higher.

For example, a £500 investment in M&G's Midland and General Unit Trust, made ten years ago, would be worth over £3,500 today. The same amount of money invested in a building society account paying an average of 10 per cent a year, net of basic rate tax, would now be worth only £1,079.

Clearly, the return from equity investments depends on how good you, or the institution or individual managing your money, are at picking shares with good prospects and avoiding the duds. So this is an area where, unless you are knowledgeable, it will pay to take independent professional advice.

Most equity-based investment schemes, whether they are unit or investment trusts, savings type life policies or direct holdings in shares, are in quoted shares – that is, companies whose shares are quoted on a stock exchange. You may buy shares in an unquoted or private company, but this can be very risky as it may be difficult to sell them.

Most individuals who hold unquoted shares do so because it is part of a family business.

Personal Equity Plans

Probably the biggest single development on the investment scene in many years has been the introduction in 1987 of PEPs (Personal Equity Plans). These carry important tax concessions and should be the first thought for anyone considering an investment in shares, unit or investment trusts.

Dividends from equities held within a PEP are completely free from income tax, while any profits made on selling the securities is free from capital gains tax. The income can be taken tax free or allowed to roll up within the PEP. You can buy and sell the shares, unit and investment trusts as often as you like, without incurring any tax liability, provided they remain within the PEP. Every PEP must have a manager: generally, this may be a life office, a bank, or a stockbroker.

You can invest up to £6,000 in the current tax year in a PEP, of which half can be in unit or investment trusts and the balance, direct investment in shares. You can have only one PEP a year; you cannot split the investment between two different PEP managers, so make sure that the PEP manager you choose offers the facility to invest in both shares and unit or investment trusts.

From January 1992, you will also be able to invest a further £3,000 a year in a 'Corporate PEP' which invests in the shares of just one company. Over a period of time, even big investors should be able to shield substantial sums from both income and capital gains tax. And the ability to take tax free income makes PEP a useful and important tool in retirement planning (See Chapter 3).

PEPs come in two kinds – the Do It Yourself variety where you choose the investments – shares, unit trusts or investment trusts – yourself, and managed PEPs. If you take the former route, the only consideration, so far as picking the PEP manager is concerned, is charges. Best buys are generally to be found amongst the smaller stockbrokers who specialize in private client business.

Independent investment advisers Chase de Vere produce an excellent guide to all the PEP schemes on offer including their terms, conditions and charges. Copies of the PEP Guide can be obtained from

Chase de Vere Investments, 63 Lincoln's Inn Fields, London WC2A 3JU. Tel: (071) 404 5766.

If you do not wish to choose the investments yourself you should opt for a managed PEP where the manager makes the investment decisions for you. In this case, it is the track record of the manager that matters much more than the charges.

An independent financial adviser will be able to recommend something suitable. Unfortunately, it is not possible to rank the comparative investment performances of the different managed PEPs on offer, because they are not directly comparable. One PEP might hold only five blue chip household name shares like Sainsbury's, Boots, Tesco, GEC and British Telecom. Another may hold a spread of UK equities as well as some foreign-invested unit trusts. You are best advised therefore to go for one of the well known investment houses with a consistent long-term investment track record.

INSURANCE LINKED SAVINGS SCHEMES

For most people, the first equity-based investment that they hold – though they may not realise it – is a with profits endowment scheme. This will probably have been sold along with a mortgage on purchasing a house or flat. This type of policy is a sound investment for the novice investor, as it removes the risk of the value of your equity holdings falling.

How does a with profits endowment work?

Premiums paid by all policyholders in the with profits fund are pooled and invested in a spread of shares, both UK and foreign, fixed interest investments and bonds as well as property. Every year, bonuses are declared and added to the value of your policy. The level of bonuses paid reflects the long-term investment performance of the fund, both past and future.

In the good years, when shares race ahead, not all the profits will be distributed in the form of bonuses. In the bad years, when shares or property go down, the fund has surpluses tucked away and is still able to pay out bonuses. Once added to a policy, these bonuses cannot be taken away so the value of your policy does not go down – it can only improve.

When the policy matures, another bonus, the terminal bonus, is also added. The split between how much is paid out in annual (or reversionary) bonuses, and the amount paid in terminal bonuses, will vary from company to company. The table below shows the bonuses paid by those life companies offering with profits endowment. It can be seen that there are wide variations in the proportion of the total payout which is attributable to reversionary bonuses compared with terminal bonuses.

The total will reflect the overall long term investment expertize of the insurance company's investment managers, and the bonus policy of the company's actuaries. Some companies are more conservative than others, preferring to keep more of their profits in reserve against a rainy day when they will have to dip into their surpluses to pay the bonuses.

The guaranteed sum assured is the amount which the policy is guaranteed to pay out should you die before the policy matures.

Benefits paid for a gross annual premium of £100, male* aged 29 at outset – 25 year term

Company	Guaranteed Sum Assured	Reversionary Bonus	Terminal Bonus	Total Maturity Value
	£	£	£	£
Britannia Life	—	—	—	—
Britannic Assurance	2381	4499	7771	14652
City of Glasgow	2745	5490	6341	14576
Clerical Medical	2321	5357	9597	17275
Co-Operative Ins	2361	3401	9965	15728
Colonial Mutual	2433	4039	7145	13617
Commercial Union	2314	10095	5274	17683
Crusader	2224	4654	6362	13240
Eagle Star	2429	8085	7600	18114
Ecclesiastical Ins	2471	4933	44443	11847
Equitable Life	2347	4546	7409	14302
Equity & Law	2385	4171	11145	17701
Friends Provident	2353	5227	10193	17773
General Accident	2326	6183	9274	17783
GRE	2395	4123	6803	13322

Company	Guaranteed Sum Assured £	Reversionary Bonus £	Terminal Bonus £	Total Maturity Value £
Legal & General	2328	6673	7674	16676
Life Assoc of Scotland	2427	3441	8948	14816
London & Manchester	2301	3870	7821	13992
London Life	2419	5058	8187	15664
Medical Sickness	2273	5351	4816	12440
MGM Assurance	2379	3170	6420	11969
National Mutual	2248	3964	8262	14474
NEL Britannia	3314	2672	4142	10128
New Ireland	2557	2971	1382	6910
Norwich Union	2389	7495	8338	18222
NPI	2537	3082	9184	14803
Pearl Assurance	2307	3620	9770	15697
Provident Mutual	2451	3668	6915	13034
Prudential Assurance	2394	5121	9708	17223
Prudential Corp.	2394	5121	9708	17223
Refuge Assurance	2326	3661	8077	14064
Reliance Mutual	2450	3438	4122	10010
RNPF for Nurses	2563	4062	10533	17158
Royal Life	2220	5972	5597	13789
Royal London Mutual	2343	6536	8752	17631
Scottish Amicable	2210	4560	10628	17398
Scottish Equitable	2247	4054	6122	12423
Scottish Life	2335	4579	9818	16732
Scottish Mutual	2415	4728	7857	15000
Scottish Provident	2272	5534	8119	15925
Scottish Widows	2208	5709	9184	17101
Standard Life	2325	4614	11796	18735
Sun Alliance	2349	5275	7517	15141
Sun Alliance	2315	5387	7494	15223
Sun Alliance	2349	5275	7517	15141
Sun Life	2379	3667	7335	13381
Sun Life of Canada	2367	3282	7061	12710
Swiss Pioneer	—	—	—	—
Tunbridge Wells Eq	2463	4299	9673	16436
Tunbridge Wells Eq	2481	14304	4673	21458

Company	Guaranteed Sum Assured	Reversionary Bonus	Terminal Bonus	Total Maturity Value
	£	£	£	£
Tunstall Assurance	2500	3906	3523	9929
Wesleyan Assurance	2374	3946	9272	15592

Source: Planned Savings Data Services
* Benefits for women would be very similar

Clearly, with so many policies to choose from, you would be well advised to take independent financial advice. The difficulty is that these savings type policies are usually linked to house purchase; also, most of the lenders are 'tied' to a life company and can only offer that life company's products. For example, Halifax Building Society is 'tied' to Standard Life and if you get a home loan from Halifax, you will be offered a Standard Life With Profits policy.

If you want impartial advice, consult an independent financial adviser before you talk to the bank or building society about a loan. There are only two major lenders who are able to give independent advice – National Westminster Bank and the Bradford & Bingley Building Society, neither of which is tied to any particular insurance company.

Unit linked life policies

These are savings type policies, similar to the with profit endowment. The difference is that the eventual payout reflects, exactly, the investment performance of the underlying shares. This is no bad thing if you can live with the ups and downs of the stock market, because the overall returns will generally be better if you pick the right policy at the outset. The table overleaf shows the relative performances of with profit and unit linked policies.

If you are going to live with this degree of risk, you may be better off with a direct investment in unit trusts or investment trusts. Charges on a unit linked life policy are much higher than on a unit or investment trust. A unit linked life policy has the flexibility to alter your investment mix and the payout on maturity is generally tax-free, although the life fund in which your premiums are invested is not tax free. Remember,

Savings and Investment

Relative performances of with profits v. unit linked policies

Gross monthly premium of £50 for male aged 29 years 11 months at outset, policy term 15 years and maturing on 1 March 1991

With Profits	£	Unit Linked Managed	£
Prudential	34,391	M&G Life	33,119
Norwich Union	34,165	Scottish Widows	29,702
Standard Life	33,692	Sun Life of Canada	25,675
Royal London Mutual	32,764	Allied Dunbar	22,877
Prudential*	32,669	Confederation Life	20,418
Refuge Assurance	32,642	London & Manchester	19,903
Eagle Star	32,296	Cannon Lincoln	18,745
Friends Provident	32,125	Barclays Life	17,945
Scottish Amicable	31,831		
Pearl	31,743		
RNPF Nurses	31,452		
Average	28,789	Average	23,548

Unit Linked (All Funds)	£
Equitable Life – UK Equity	36,368
Friends Provident – UK Equity	33,587
M&G Life – Managed	33,119
Confederation Life – UK Equity	30,069
Scottish Widows – Managed	29,702
Allied Dunbar – UK Equity	27,168
Equity & Law – UK Equity	26,648
Sun Life of Canada – Managed	25,675
Cannon Lincoln – UK Equity	24,839
M&G Life – UK Equity	24,414
Average	23,142

* Pru bonuses revised 1/4/91 producing a lower maturity.
Source: Planned Savings Data Services

however, that there are heavy penalties if you surrender in the first five years. A unit trust fund pays no capital gains tax – but you may be liable to CGT on any profits you take.

Unit linked insurance company bonds are lump sum investments and should only be considered if your special circumstances demand them. Always seek independent advice.

Unit and investment trusts – pooled investments
For the novice investor who has already got a with profits endowment

and wants to take the plunge into direct investment in shares, the safest way to invest is through pooled investments such as unit or investment trusts.

Both invest in a spread of shares and reduce the risk through their multiple holdings. If you hold a single share and the company fails, you lose everything. If you invest in twenty different companies, some may do well, others not so well and one may collapse, but you have reduced the risk.

Unit and investment trusts may invest in a particular geographical area like the UK or North America, the Far East or Australia, or in different sectors of the market such as oil or mining companies, income stocks or recovery situations. Each individual fund has specific investment objectives. In building up a portfolio of these trusts, you will need to choose a selection, both geographically, and in terms of the type of fund.

With over 1,349 unit trusts on offer as well as 254 investment trusts, you will clearly need independent advice on which trusts to pick.

There are significant differences between unit and investment trusts. Unit trusts are open-ended funds, while investment trusts are closed funds. With a unit trust the money from small investors is pooled and a spread of shares is bought. Each day, the underlying shares in the fund are valued and the total is divided by the number of units which have been issued to investors. The price of these units, whether buying or selling, is determined by the price of the underlying investments, less any management charges.

An investment trust is different. It is an investment company with shares quoted on the Stock Exchange. The price of a share reflects to some extent the value of the underlying investments, but it is also affected by the supply and demand for the investment trusts shares. In recent years, most investment trusts have been trading at a discount to the value of the underlying investments. The assets may be worth 100p per share, but you could buy the investment trusts shares at, say, 90p. There have, however, been periods when they have traded at a premium. This adds another variable to the equation which has to be taken into account.

If you have not used your PEP allowance for the current tax year, any investment in unit or investment trusts should be put into a PEP to shield it from income tax and CGT.

Regular savings

Many unit trusts and investment trusts run regular savings schemes to encourage the small investor. This is a very good way of building up an equity holding over a period of time and is much cheaper and more flexible than the with profits endowment and unit linked life policies. If you need cash in a hurry, you can sell some of the units and there are no penalties. Should you find yourself in difficulties over keeping up the monthly payments you can stop, without penalty, and continue at a later date. In addition, you can add lump sums at any time.

The Unit Trust Association or the Association of Investment Trust Companies (see page 152 for more details) can provide you with a list of those fund managers that run regular savings schemes.

Choosing a trust

With over 1,349 unit trusts and 254 investment trusts to choose from specializing in everything from esoteric commodity shares to companies with household names, picking a unit or investment trust can be a nightmare. If you want to do it yourself, read the personal finance pages of the quality national daily newspapers which regularly look at unit and investment trusts and give details of past performance.

This is another area where it will clearly pay to take independent advice. Some independent financial advisers specialize almost exclusively in unit and investment trusts and will recommend a portfolio of funds tailored to suit your needs.

The investment returns from all investment and unit trusts are independently monitored by Micropal. While this statistical service is too detailed and probably too expensive for the average small investor, Micropal can give you the names of financial advisers in your area who take their service.

Sadly, neither the Unit Trust Association nor the Association of Investment Trust Companies, the two trade associations, can, as yet, produce a list of specialist brokers.

Buying and selling

Unit trusts can be bought and sold direct through the managers. You do not need a stockbroker or other intermediary unless you want advice on which trusts to buy.

Charges for buying and selling are included in what is known as the 'spread'. Nearly all unit trusts have two prices, 'bid' and 'offer'. The bid price is the price at which the managers will buy back your units. The offer price is the price which you have to pay when you buy. The 'spread' is the difference between the bid and offer price—usually five to six per cent.

For example, if you were to buy units at an offer price of 100p and sell them again an hour later (not something one would normally do), you would find that the bid price was only 94p or 95p. The charges would have eaten up five per cent of your money.

Investment trusts are quoted shares and can be bought through a stockbroker or one of the high street bank's sharedealing services. Commission is charged; on average the minimum is around £20. For bargains over £1,000, you will probably pay the old Stock Exchange rate of 1.67 per cent, diminishing as the size of the investment increases. With the deregulation of the Stock Exchange, fixed commissions have gone, so it pays to shop around. Generally speaking, the cheapest deals are from 'execution only' brokers like Sharelink or the services operated by the smaller private client stockbrokers.

Direct investment in shares

If you want to invest directly in shares, you will either have to pick the companies yourself, or you will need a sizeable lump sum – an absolute minimum of £50,000 – before a stockbroker will be interested in managing a portfolio for you. Below £50,000, virtually all stockbrokers will put you into unit or investment trusts.

However, if you are prepared to take the plunge on your own, there are several sharedealing services and stockbrokers who offer an 'execution only' service at very cheap rates.

Most private client stockbrokers will offer an 'execution only' sharedealing service if asked, although few actively promote it. Sharelink (dealing tel: (021) 200 2474) is the only sharedealing service which is both comprehensive and available to everybody. Minimum commission starts as low as £12.50 per bargain, if you are prepared to deal by post, £17.50 for telephone dealing and £20 for the full private client service.

NatWest Bank offers a touchscreen sharedealing service through 275 of its branches and this is available to non-customers. At the moment it is limited to the top 500 shares but this covers all the major companies.

Norwich & Peterborough Building Society offers a full execution only service through its 67 branches and is available to all.

Don't feel intimidated at the thought of having a flutter in shares, even if you are not entirely sure what to go for. An absolute beginner can have a lot of fun punting in shares, provided you treat it a bit like putting money on the favourite in the 3.30 pm at Sandown. Unlike horseracing, however, you would be very unlucky to lose everything. Share prices do go up and down, sometimes wildly. But only a very small proportion of companies go bust and leave you with absolutely nothing.

Tax

You will pay tax on some types of equity-linked investments. Dividends on shares, unit and investment trusts are all subject to income tax and have basic rate tax deducted at source. A non-taxpayer can reclaim this. However, dividends are tax-free if the securities are held within a PEP, which is the sensible thing to do.

Profits on selling shares, unit or investment trusts, whether lump sum investments or regular savings, are subject to CGT at either 25 per cent or 40 per cent, depending on the rate of income tax you pay. However, the first £5,500 (1991-92) of profits realised each year are exempt. In addition, if you have losses from previous years, these can be carried forward and offset against profits. By using the exemption, even those with quite a large portfolio of investments can avoid CGT. Securities held within a PEP are free from CGT.

The payout from a with profit endowment or other savings type policy is generally tax-free, provided you have paid the premiums for at least ten years, or for three-quarters of the term of the policy – but the investments will have been subject to tax within the life company's fund. There could, however, be a liability to higher rate tax on encashment of some life policies or on early surrender. If in doubt, ask your professional adviser.

Business Expansion Scheme

The BES was introduced in 1983 and was designed to give small investors an incentive to invest in small companies which generally have difficulty in obtaining finance from elsewhere.

Currently, you can get tax relief at your highest rate paid on up to £40,000 a year invested in BES companies, and any profits on sale after five years are free from CGT.

By their nature, BES companies are higher-risk investments because they are small companies, generally in a start-up situation. Surveys show that one in three of all new businesses started will not survive the first five years. However, if you are prepared to take the risk, the potential rewards can be great. And if all else fails, you have at least had the tax relief.

BES companies are restricted in the amount of money they can raise to £750,000, unless they are a property company building, or developing, property for private rental, in which case the limit is £5 million.

Because of the costs involved in setting up a BES company, the low maximum of £750,000 has deterred the vast majority of trading companies from raising finance through this route. As a result, most of the BES schemes on offer in recent years have been assured tenancy schemes. Depending on your view of property prices and the rental market, these may be considered less risky than trading companies. Even if the property market were to collapse, there would still be some value to the properties held within the BES company.

There are two publications which monitor all the BES issues as they are offered – The *BES Magazine* and *BESt Investment*. They evaluate the degree of risk involved and the expertise of the management as well as the charging structure. If you want to invest in a BES company, you would be well advised to subscribe to one of these publications or to take advice from an independent intermediary.

Conclusion

Investment can be fun – even if you prefer to keep most of your money in a building society, there is no reason why you should not have a flutter in a few shares. But always remember: do not gamble with money you cannot afford to lose. And for the novice, there is no doubt that it pays to take independent advice.

The Stock Exchange (see Useful Addresses on page 153) will supply a list of stockbrokers prepared to take on new private clients. IFA Promotions, which represents independent financial advisers, will supply the names of IFAs in your area.

PENSIONS

Saving for retirement is something many people try to avoid thinking about – very often until it is too late. But if you believe that you will be able to do anything more than subsist on the State retirement pension, then you are not facing reality.

State retirement pension

State retirement pension currently stands at £52 a week for a single person, £83.25 a week for a married couple, and you are entitled to the maximum only if you have the requisite National Insurance contributions. You don't need to be a mathematical wizard to work out that retirement is not going to be much fun if you rely entirely on the basic State pension for income.

You may be entitled to a higher pension if you have paid contributions to SERPS, the State Earnings Related Pension Scheme, or if between 1961 and April 1975 you paid graduated contributions – but it is not a lot more.

Given that the average earnings of female full-time employees is only £10,500, even if you qualify for the maximum SERPS addition, life may still be tough financially.

Of course, not everyone is eligible for the maximum benefits. To qualify for the full basic State pension, you must have made National Insurance contributions or been credited with them for 39 years out of the 44 between the ages of sixteen and sixty, if you are a woman, or 44 years out of the 49 between the ages of sixteen and sixty-five, if you are a man.

Clearly, anyone who goes to university or embarks upon a higher education course will instantly have difficulty in qualifying for the full pension. Women who subsequently have career breaks to have children, or those who do not work after they are married will find it still harder to earn the maximum pension.

However, if you are married, you may be entitled to a State retirement pension based on your husband's earnings. Working wives can qualify in their own right.

The State Earnings Related Pension Scheme – in or out?

SERPS was introduced in 1978 as a means of topping up the basic State pension, and the intention was to provide the average employee on average earnings with a reasonable level of State pension. This would be made up of the basic State pension and the SERPS supplement. Unfortunately, this aim has not been been achieved and SERPS benefit has had to be substantially reduced.

With an ageing population, it rapidly became apparent that the cost of providing this benefit would be more than the working population could bear. The problem is that SERPS is a pay-as-you-go scheme. Part of the National Insurance contributions of those working today are used to pay the benefits to those who are retired.

The number of pensioners as a proportion of the population is rising and by the turn of the century is expected to reach 10 million; by the year 2035, it could reach 13 million. The number of people working in the UK will fall from 2.3 per pensioner to 1.6; clearly, National Insurance contributions will have to rise dramatically if the promised SERPS benefits are to be paid.

In fact, it was the high cost of SERPS that prompted the Government to introduce personal pensions in 1988, with the option of getting out of SERPS and making a private pension provision, but primarily personal pensions were introduced to encourage individual provision and privatization.

To encourage people to do this, the Government offered the incentive of a rebate of that part of your National Insurance contributions which represents the funding of SERPS, plus a two per cent bonus, which the Government will pay into your pension plan each year until 5 April 1993.

For the vast majority of employees who are members of an occupational pension scheme, the decision is simple – do nothing. Most occupational pension schemes are already contracted out of SERPS. The company pension scheme has already taken the NI rebate and will provide benefits at least as good as those you would enjoy under SERPS.

But for those employees who are not members of an occupational pension scheme or for those who belong to a 'contracted in' occupational scheme, you have to decide whether to opt out of SERPS or not.

Some five million employees have already opted to do so. The self-employed do not have to worry, since they are not eligible to join SERPS in the first place and therefore cannot contract out.

Broadly speaking, if you are over 40 it will pay to remain within SERPS – if you are under 40, it may pay you to opt out and put the National Insurance rebate plus the two per cent bonus into a personal pension. The calculations behind this broad rule are complicated and it is not necessary to understand the detail.

At the moment, you have the option to go back into SERPS and if you have already opted out, say at the age of 27 three years ago, it will be to your advantage to opt back into SERPS at the age of 40. Ask your pension adviser if you are in any doubt.

Employees who are members of a 'contracted in' pension scheme can take out a personal pension for the sole purpose of contracting out of SERPS, yet remain within the occupational pension scheme. This is called a 'rebate only' personal pension, because the contributions consist entirely of the National Insurance rebate plus the two per cent incentive. This is one of two situations where you are allowed to contribute to both a personal pension and an occupational pension at the same time. The other is if you have two sources of income—one which is pensionable under an occupational scheme, the other which is not.

It is self-evident that with the State pension worth so little, everyone should make extra provision for their retirement—either through an occupational pension scheme, personal pension, or another form of long term saving such as a Personal Equity Plan.

If there is one golden rule with planning for retirement, it should be that the sooner you start, the better.

Women have different pension requirements from men because they live longer, retire earlier and frequently have fewer years when they are earning to build up pension rights or save for retirement.

The effect of career breaks on pensions is dramatic. A woman who works all her adult life will generally have to contribute around 10 per cent more to a pension scheme than a man because she will probably retire five years before her male counterpart. If she also takes just five years off to have children, or for some other reason, she will have to contribute up to 50 per cent more to a pension scheme than a man. However, the sooner she starts, the better, because any contributions made prior to a career break will begin to build up towards a reasonable pension.

If you have no earnings, the only way to provide for retirement is to save long term in something like a Personal Equity Plan, unit or investment trust regular savings scheme, with profits endowment policy or a similar equity-based investment. You are not eligible to contribute to a personal pension unless you have earnings. See Chapter 2, page 39 on Savings.

OCCUPATIONAL PENSIONS

There are over 11 million employees who are members of an occupational pension scheme run by their employers. If you are employed, there is a good chance that you will have the opportunity to become a member of such a scheme. Generally speaking, if you have not already joined, it will pay to become a member. The reason is straightforward.

Final salary scheme

There are two types of occupational pension scheme – final salary and money purchase. The vast majority of employees in occupational pension schemes are in final salary schemes and will, typically, enjoy a pension of one-sixtieth of their salary at the date of retirement, for every year of employment.

For the person who works for forty years with the same firm, this works out at 40/60ths or two-thirds of your final salary at retirement age – the maximum permitted by the Inland Revenue.

More than nine out of ten company pension schemes are final salary schemes and a large percentage of them offer one-sixtieth of final salary, or better, for every year of service.

Most employers contribute a significant amount to the company pension scheme; 15 per cent of each member's salary is not uncommon. Employees, on average, are asked to contribute about five per cent of their salary. Clearly, any pension scheme where there are two contributions – one from you and one from your employer – is likely to produce better benefits than a personal pension plan where you alone will make contributions.

In addition, the employer guarantees the benefits of a final salary scheme. If you were to reach retirement age and the pension scheme did not have sufficient money to pay your pension as promised, the employer would have to pay up. In fact this is most unlikely to happen because pension schemes are reviewed regularly to ensure that there are sufficient assets to meet the fund's liabilities. If there are not, then the employer makes an extra contribution to cover the shortfall. Your employer has to pick up the bill and effectively 'guarantees' the pension. Very occasionally, when a company has been in difficulties, future pension benefits have been reduced, but this is unusual. The benefits earned to date, however, cannot be changed.

So find out if your employer has a pension scheme and whether you are eligible to join. Ask if it is final salary, or money purchase, because this could affect your decision too.

Money purchase scheme

Money purchase, as the name indicates, means that your pension benefits are related to the amount of money paid in contributions, both by you and by your employer, and how well they are invested. The pension paid at retirement will not necessarily bear any relationship to the salary you are earning at retirement.

Smaller firms tend to run money purchase schemes, because the employer's liability is limited entirely to the contributions he decides to make. If the pension at retirement bears no relation to the salary you are earning and is insufficient to live on, he has no obligation to do anything about it.

But here again, provided your employer is making worthwhile contributions to the scheme, it will still pay you to join on the basis that two contributions are better than one. You should also bear in mind that you will probably be eligible for death-in-service benefits and, more importantly, your employer will probably increase his contributions to account for cost of living increases. Only if your employer's contribution is negligible or non-existent should you consider going it alone with a personal pension.

The choice is important because once you join the company pension scheme you will not be eligible to make contributions to a personal pension plan. However you will be able to top up your pension with an AVC (Additional Voluntary Contribution). Your employer may run one alongside the main pension fund. Alternatively, you are entitled to go to an insurance company and purchase a freestanding AVC yourself.

One of the major disadvantages of occupational pensions has now largely been removed – at least for employees who have joined a company scheme since 1978. Although a good pension scheme offers two-thirds final salary at retirement age, in the past only those employees who stayed with one firm all their working lives ever qualified for this maximum pension. Those who changed jobs were heavily penalized for making the move and the investment returns on their frozen contributions were used to pay for better benefits for those who stayed. But since 1985, pension benefits earned by a former employee subsequent to that date must be uprated in line with the lesser of the rate of inflation, or five per cent. Job changers are no longer heavily penalized, so if you can join an occupational scheme, do so, safe in the knowledge that you will get a fair deal if you decide to move or transfer jobs.

Additional Voluntary Contributions

Although there is now a considerable amount of protection for the pension benefits of job changers, the fact remains that there are many employees who will not have earned enough pension benefits in their company scheme to retire in comfort.

One answer is to make extra contributions to an Additional Voluntary Contributions (AVC) scheme. Since October 1987, employees have enjoyed the absolute right to make contributions to Free Standing AVC schemes (FSAVCs) – not just the AVC run by their employer. This means that you can belong to your company's pension scheme, but buy an AVC in your own name from a life company.

There is one potential drawback with AVCs: if you joined an AVC scheme prior to 7 April 1987, you will be able to take a proportion of the benefits at retirement as a tax-free cash lump sum – just as you can with the main pension benefits. Since that date, however, anyone taking out a new AVC cannot take any benefits as cash; the contributions can only buy a pension.

However, in reality this is only a notional restriction because the pension benefits earned by your AVC are taken into account when calculating the maximum lump sum which can be taken from the main pension scheme.

For example, you may retire on a final salary of £24,000. Your main pension scheme pays you a pension of £8,000. Because the pension is less than the Inland Revenue's permitted maximum of two-thirds final salary, the lump sum which you can take at retirement is restricted to £18,000. But your AVC might produce an annual pension of, say, £4,000 a year. This brings your total pension benefits up to £12,000 a year and allows the main pension to pay you a lump sum of £27,000, assuming you have no pension from any other source.

You are entitled to full tax relief on contributions to an AVC or an FSAVC. There is a ceiling on this tax relief of 15 per cent of earnings and you must include in this 15 per cent any deductions made at source from your pay for contributions to the main occupational pension scheme.

A large number of life offices offer FSAVCs, and you can invest in anything from a straight deposit account to the usual range of managed, equity, fixed interest and property funds. There are also straight building society deposit schemes and with profits type AVCs.

The vast majority of employees investing in AVCs choose a straight deposit fund, if they are only a few years off retirement, or a managed fund if they have more than five years to go.

The table shows the amount you need to contribute to an AVC or an FSAVC at various ages to bring your pension entitlement up to the maximum permitted by the Inland Revenue – two-thirds of your final salary, assuming that your pension scheme provides half of your final salary.

The figures assume current earnings of £25,500, rising by 8.5 per cent a year, and a retirement age of 65, that the invested contributions

Contribution levels for AVCs and FSAVCs

Age Next Birthday	Pension Scheme Final Salary	Actual Final Salary	Inland Revenue Maximum Pension	Scheme Pension	AVC % to fund deficiency
	£	£	£	£	%
25	454,890	694,135	462,756	227,445	4.73
30	302,522	461,630	307,753	151,261	5.87
35	201,191	307,005	204,670	100,595	7.44
40	133,801	204,172	136,114	66,900	9.65
45	88,984	135,784	90,522	44,492	12.65
50	59,178	90,302	60,201	29,589	18.54*

* *This would exceed the maximum allowable for tax relief.*

will grow by 12 per cent a year and that the member of the scheme will have twenty years' service to retirement age.

Choosing an AVC scheme is very much like choosing a personal pension. There is a wide variety on offer with differing investment track records. You will need to consult an independent financial adviser who specializes in pensions to choose the option that best suits your own circumstances.

PERSONAL PENSIONS

- *What is a personal pension?*
Personal pensions are long-term savings contracts, issued by life assurance companies, friendly societies, unit trust groups, banks, building societies and other financial institutions. They can provide a combination of a tax-free lump sum and pension at retirement. The benefits can only be paid out on retirement or on death before retirement age: money cannot otherwise be withdrawn.

- *How does a personal pension work?*
Personal pensions and their predecessor, Self Employed Retirement Annuities (SERAs) are 'defined contribution' schemes—in other words, what you get out in terms of pension at retirement reflects how much you have put in, and how well that money has been invested.

Most large occupational pension schemes are 'defined benefit' schemes, which means that the benefits to be paid at retirement are set out in the trust deed and the employer then has to pay sufficient into the fund to provide the promised pensions.

All personal pension plans are basically the same. You pay your contributions into a tax-free pension fund, which may invest in anything from equities to fixed interest securities and property.

A share of the investment profits are allocated to your personal pension policy and at retirement age the accumulated contributions plus profits are used to purchase the benefits – an annuity, or income for life. You also have the option of taking part of the accumulated fund as a tax-free lump sum, and it is nearly always in your best interest to do so.

You can make regular contributions to a personal pension contract, or one-off lump sums, or both. Tax relief at your highest rate of income tax paid is allowed on contributions, and the investment fund into which these contributions are paid is also free of tax. This means that investments can accumulate at a faster rate than in, say, a life assurance savings contract where profits and dividends are taxed within the life fund.

The size of the accumulated fund allocated to your pension policy depends on how well the life company invests the contributions, and what administration charges have been deducted from the value of the underlying investments.

Once paid in, money cannot be withdrawn from a personal pension until you reach retirement age. At retirement, you have the option of a pension, which is treated as taxable income, or you can take a lower pension and a tax-free lump sum of up to 25 per cent of the accumulated fund. With Self Employed Retirement Annuities (SERAs), which preceded the introduction of personal pensions, it was possible to take a slightly larger tax-free proportion as a lump sum, so if you have existing SERAs, it is well worthwhile continuing with them.

If you have dependants, you can arrange for a pension to be paid to them on your death. This typically might be one-third, a half or two-thirds of the main pension paid to you. Clearly, there is a price to pay for this. Broadly speaking, to provide a dependant's pension of two-thirds of the basic pension will cost around 20 per cent of the accumulated fund at retirement.

Where there are no dependants, you can opt for a larger pension at retirement age and for the accumulated contributions plus any increase in their value to be paid to your estate, should you die before retirement. Generally speaking, if you die after retirement and haven't chosen a pension which is payable to your dependants, all benefits die with you unless you have opted to protect the benefits for up to ten years. But here again there is a price to pay in the form of a lower pension at retirement age. It is also worth considering taking a lower pension, but having the benefits index-linked. What may seem a comfortable income when you first retire, could look hopelessly inadequate ten years later.

– *Who is eligible?*

Anyone who has earnings and who is not a member of an occupational pension scheme is entitled to make contributions to a personal pension plan. If you are a member of your company pension scheme but have other part-time earnings, you can make contributions to a personal pension in relation to your part-time earnings. The biggest group of individuals who contribute to personal pensions are the self-employed.

– *Tax relief*

Personal pensions are the most tax-efficient way to save long term for your retirement, because you are entitled to claim relief at your highest rate of income tax paid on contributions made. The table overleaf shows the maximum amount which can be contributed at various ages.

In 1989, the Chancellor of the Exchequer put an upper limit on the amount of earnings which could be taken into account when calculating tax relief on pensions contributions. For 1989-90 it was £60,000 and since then it has been increased in line with inflation to £71,400. You are not eligible for tax relief on pension contributions on earnings above this ceiling.

If you are a really high earner, you can top up your pension with Personal Equity Plans (PEPs). There is no tax relief on money invested in a PEP, but the income from the investments, and any capital gains, are completely tax-free, which can be very useful in retirement planning. You can invest in growth shares while you are working and convert the investments to high income shares, unit or investment trusts

Maximum contributions to a personal pension/retirement annuity*

Age on 6 April	*% of Net Relevant Earnings*		
	PERSONAL PENSIONS		RETIREMENT ANNUITIES
	1988-89	*1989-92*	*1987-92*
35 or less	17.5	17.5	17.5
36-45	17.5	20.0	17.5
46-50	17.5	25.0	17.5
51-55	20.0	30.0	20.0
56-60	22.5	35.0	22.5
61-74	27.5	40.0	27.5
Life Assurance	5.0	5.0	5.0

* *Personal pensions, introduced in 1988, were preceded by Self Employed Retirement Annuities (SERAs).*

Maximum tax relief for personal pensions in cash terms

Age on 6 April	*% of Net Relevant Earnings*		
	1989-90	*1990-91*	*1991-92*
	£	£	£
35 or less	10,500	11,340	12,495
36-45	12,000	12,960	14,280
46-50	15,000	16,200	17,850
51-55	18,000	19,440	21,420
56-60	21,000	22,680	24,990
61-74	24,000	25,920	28,560

Maximum pensionable earnings for personal pensions and retirement annuities

	1989-90	*1990-91*	*1991-92*
	£	£	£
	60,000	64,800	71,400

Retirement Annuities Contribution Limits 1982-87
Born after 1933 — 17.5%
Born 1916-1933 — 20.0%

at retirement, and enjoy a tax-free income. PEPs also have the advantage of allowing you to keep control of your money. See page 56 for a full description of PEPs.

You can backdate your pension contributions to the previous tax year or the year before, and it may be advantageous to do so if you were paying tax at a higher rate during those years.

You are also entitled to catch up and carry forward unused pension tax relief for up to six years if in previous years you could not afford to make the maximum contributions to a pension scheme – and very few people can. In order to take advantage of this, you must have paid the maximum contributions for the current tax year or the previous year.

The rules are complicated, but any pensions adviser or accountant will make the calculation for you.

Basic rate tax relief on pension premiums is given in the same way as mortgage interest relief – it is deducted at source. Higher rate taxpayers will get further tax relief by claiming through the yearly tax assessment. If you are self-employed, you will pay gross contributions and obtain all your tax relief through your tax assessment.

When the pension starts to be paid at retirement, it is treated as earned income and taxed in the usual way.

– How much should I contribute to a personal pension?

If you want to retire on a realistic pension, the answer is as much as you can afford and the sooner you start, the better. The maximum pension allowable from an occupational pension scheme is two-thirds of your final salary. But there are two contributions to an occupational scheme – the employee's and the employer's. If you are making your own retirement provision through a personal pension, the income you receive when you retire is entirely dependent on the level of your contributions.

The table overleaf shows the percentage of earnings you would need to save in a personal pension to achieve the same level of pension as an employee in a good company scheme – two-thirds of your final salary.

The figures assume that money invested in the personal pension plan shows an average return of 8.5 per cent a year. Salary and contributions are assumed to increase by an average of 6.5 per cent a year and no cash is taken from the personal pension plan at retirement age.

Given that most people have very little money to save while they are

**Contributions as a percentage of income needed to produce
a pension of two-thirds final salary**

Initial salary £10,000		
Age Now	Retirement Age	
	60	65
30	18.9%	14.1%
35	23.6%	17.2%
40	30.8%	21.6%
45	42.6%	28.2%
50	66.3%	39.1%
55	129.5%	61.1%

young and on relatively low earnings, or during the time when they are bringing up children, it is obvious that most savings for retirement will be done after the age of 45. By this time, as the table shows, the sums of money that you need to invest to provide a realistic pension are high so it is almost impossible to save too much.

Choosing a personal pension

Pensions are complicated, and you will almost certainly need professional help in choosing the right plan. You should definitely consult an independent financial adviser, who will be able to analyse your needs and suggest a suitable solution.

For example, you may be buying a personal pension, but what should you do about the benefits which are locked up in the pension scheme of a former employer? Or perhaps you run your own business. An independent adviser will provide a number of solutions to pension provision.

However, it will pay to understand the basics so that you know what it is you are buying and what benefits the pension policies will provide.

With profits versus unit linked pensions

Personal pensions come in two basic types: with profits pensions, which offer a certain level of guarantee, and unit linked pensions, which don't.

With the former, your contributions are held within a fund which invests in a mixture of shares, fixed interest securities and property. Bonuses are added to your pension policy to reflect the overall long-term investment performance of the fund, but not all the profits are paid out. During good years, when the fund is showing handsome gains, some are retained so that bonuses can be paid to policyholders during the leaner years.

However, once these bonuses have been declared, they are added to your policy and cannot be taken away. This means that the value of your pension policy can only go up – it cannot go down.

These with profits pension policies offer a reasonable degree of security, and some offer a guaranteed minimum bonus rate, but they do not necessarily provide the best return.

To obtain a potentially better return from a personal pension you have to be prepared to take a higher risk with a unit linked plan. These are very similar to unit trusts. Your contributions are paid into a fund which may invest in shares, fixed interest securities, property or a mixture of all three.

The fund is 'unitised' and a number of units are allocated to your pension plan. For example, if the value of the underlying investments in the fund is £1 million and there are 100,000 units issued, then the value of each unit will be £10. The value of your units will reflect the underlying investment performance of the fund.

It is important to fully understand the implications of this. For example, people coming up to retirement age in the autumn of 1987 might have had widely varying experiences in terms of pension benefits paid out on a unit linked pension policy. If they took their benefits before the stock market crash of October 1987, they might well have been 30 per cent or more better off than someone retiring in, say, December 1987. Share prices worldwide dropped dramatically and this would have been reflected in the value of units held in a unitised pension fund.

However, it is also true that unit linked pension plans can show a much higher return than the more cautious with profits type. Also, there are ways of crystallising gains made in a unit linked pension fund by transferring units into a safe cash or fixed interest fund in the years before retirement.

Most unit linked pension policies offer a choice of funds into which your contributions can be channelled, and you are able to switch funds, depending on your investment objectives. However, very few individuals do actually switch their money around, although some independent financial advisers offer a management service, making the switching decisions for you. Some life offices will also offer you the chance to switch between with profits and unit linked policies.

The funds offered by the life company will generally include a managed fund which invests in equities, fixed interest securities and property as well as a wide range of specialist funds investing in everything from the Far Eastern markets to the USA and from large-scale commodity shares to the smaller companies.

The point to grasp is that personal pensions, like savings-type life policies, are all about investment performance. The better the investments perform, the greater the accumulated fund at retirement age, and the higher the benefits.

The table below shows the accumulated fund from the top ten with profits type contracts.

Actual Results

Accumulated Fund available to male aged 65 on 1st June 1990 or 31st May 1991 for a gross annual premium of £500. Policy effected by male aged 44 yrs 11 mths or male aged 54 yrs 11 mths. *

	20 YEAR CONTRACT		10 YEAR CONTRACT		
1990					
Company	*Accumulated Cash Fund*	*Premium Returned* **	*Company*	*Accumulated Cash Fund*	*Premium Returned* **
Norwich Union	76,104	RNI	Pearl	16,837	3.5%
Scottish Provident	73,092	RWI	Clerical Medical	16,820	RNI
Equitable Life	71,128	ROF	Scottish Amicable	16,232	RNI
Legal & General	69,874	RNI	Sun Alliance	16,047	RNI
Provident Mutual	69,033	ROF	Norwich Union	16,017	RNI
National Provident	68,837	RWI	Friends Provident	15,873	RNI
Scottish Life	68,128	5%	Sentinel Life	15,850	RNI
Equity & Law	67,400	RNI	Equitable Life	15,830	ROF
Sun Life	66,430	RNI	London Life	15,536	ROF
Scottish Widows	65,505	RNI	Equity & Law	15,463	RNI

20 YEAR CONTRACT			10 YEAR CONTRACT		
1991					
Company	Accumu-lated Cash Fund	Premium Returned**	Company	Accumu-lated Cash Fund	Premium Returned**
Norwich Union	79,102	RNI	Friends Provident	15,875	RNI
Scottish Widows	77,872	RNI	Sentinel Life	15,850	RNI
GRE	75,218	RNI	Eagle Star	15,831	RNI
Prudential	73,604	4%	Scottish Mutual	15,786	RNI
Equitable Life	71,376	ROF	Pearl	15,776	3.5%
National Provident	70,899	RWI	Norwich Union	15,629	RNI
Scottish Life	70,130	5%	Scottish Amicable	15,288	RNI
Scottish Provident	69,978	RWI	Clerical Medical	14,630	RNI
Provident Mutual	69,225	ROF	National Mutual	14,568	ROF
Sun Life	66,783	RNI	Commercial Union	14,513	RNI

Equitable Life: ROF since 1/9/79, RWI prior to 1/9/79
* Figures for females would be comparable to these figures.
** On death before retirement.
Source: Planned Savings Data Services

RNI - Return No Interest
RWI - Return With Interest
ROF - Return of Full Accumulated Fund

– *Which do you choose?*

A belt and braces approach is probably the best, unless you are only a few years off retirement, or you are the worrying kind and cannot live with the more risky unit linked type of policy.

You might decide on a with profits policy for, say, one-third of your pension contributions, with the balance in unit linked schemes with a broad spread of investments.

The younger you are and the further off retirement, the more you can afford to take risks because there is plenty of time for a downturn in the world's stockmarkets to reverse itself before you retire. Anyone with twenty years or more to go to retirement could probably afford to put all their contributions in unit linked funds and switch to with profits schemes nearer to retirement. But remember, while the best performing unit linked schemes generally out-perform the best with profits pension plans, there is no guarantee that you will pick the right one; the worst performing unit linked schemes can be much worse than the worst with profits schemes.

Single premium or regular premium?

You can put your money into a personal pension, either as single premium lump sums or as regular monthly contributions, or both. Single premiums are the most cost-effective, as the charges are lower. They are also more flexible, allowing you to pay as much or as little as you can afford with no future commitment.

This is particularly important for anyone who is self-employed and may have fluctuating earnings. Also, because unused pension tax relief can be carried forward for up to six years, you are not missing out.

Regular premium contracts have higher charges, so less of your money is invested. But they do have the advantage of imposing a discipline if you are bad at saving. With regular contributions to unit linked pensions, you have the benefit of 'pound cost averaging' – your contributions buy more units when prices are low, less when they are high, which tends to even out the return. A good regular premium policy will allow you to make additional, one-off lump sum payments.

If your personal pension is linked to the repayment of a home loan, you will generally find that the lender requires you to make regular pension contributions.

Questions to ask your pensions adviser

– What benefits will the plan give my dependants?

Most policies allow you to tailor the dependant's pension to your particular need and will provide a dependant's pension of, say, one-third or a half of the main pension. If both you and your partner are investing in personal pensions, it is better for you to make contributions in your own name, rather than relying on the dependant's pension from your partner's pension. The benefits are better.

– What happens if I die before retirement?

A good pension policy will offer the return of the accumulated fund including profits up to the date of your death. If you are a single parent, these benefits should be written in trust for the benefit of your children to avoid inheritance tax.

– What happens if I am sick and unable to pay the premiums?
Almost all pensions offer a waiver of premiums as an option which will
pay the pension premiums during this period.

– At what age can I retire?
You can take your pension at any age between 50 and 75 – certain
categories of people like jockeys, footballers and other sportsmen and
women are allowed to retire earlier.

If you know absolutely that you want to retire at, say, 60, make sure
that the pension plan is written to that age, not older, as charges on
any regular pension plan are based on the time that the plan still has
left to run.

With the old SERAs, retirement can be taken between the ages of
60 and 75. Check whether there is any penalty imposed for early
retirement.

– What life assurance cover can be included?
Investors in personal pensions and SERAs are entitled to tax relief on
life assurance premiums written in conjunction with a personal pension.
You can contribute up to five per cent of earnings for this benefit. This
is very useful for providing dependant's benefits.

– What happens if I cannot afford to keep up the premiums?
You generally have the option of making a pension policy 'paid up'
– like a life policy. A good policy will also offer the option of reinstating
payments if the inability to pay is only temporary, due to, perhaps, a
period of unemployment. Also, do bear in mind too that you might need
to make a policy paid up because you have changed jobs and have
decided to join the new employer's pension scheme. Check if there are
any penalties.

You should also ask if the pension has the option both to reduce and
increase premiums. Some policies offer the option of index-linking both
premiums and benefits. This can be arranged for you at no charge.

**– Will the pension policy allow me to make lump sum
contributions as well as regular payments?**
This is a useful option if you want to boost your pension with a one-off
lump sum investment.

– *Can the pension policy take transfer payments?*

You may have deferred pension benefits in the occupational pension scheme of a former employer which you want to transfer into the personal pension. Check that it has this facility.

– *What are the options on retirement?*

Most personal pensions offer a variety of options on retirement. You can take up to 25 per cent of the accumulated fund as tax-free cash (one-third if it is one of the old pre-1988 SERAs). If you decide that you need protection from inflation, you can opt for an index-linked pension, although this will mean that the benefit will start at lower than the usual level.

You can also alter the dependant's benefits. Your partner may have inherited some money, for example, and there is no longer a requirement for a dependant's pension. This will mean that you can take a higher pension. You might also want to postpone retirement or phase it in. Ask if the pension policy offers these options. A number of companies offer 'cluster' policies. Some policies within the 'cluster' can be used at, say, age 60 to supplement income if you decide to work part time rather than retire fully. The others are used at a later date. This is also a useful way of organizing your own 'index linking' to take account of inflation.

If you want the payment of pension protected, this is generally an option for anything up to the first ten years. But you will have to accept a lower initial pension.

Personal pensions v. occupational schemes

– *Advantages of personal pensions*

● Portable – personal pensions can be taken with you from job to job and maintained through periods of self-employment. There is no loss of benefit on changing jobs.
● Flexible – they can be tailored to your specific needs in terms of both contributions and benefits.
● Convenient – they can accept transfer payments from the pension scheme run by a former employer, thereby keeping all of your pension in one place.

– *Disadvantages of personal pensions*

- More expensive – to provide a comfortable living in retirement through a personal pension, you will have to pay much more than if you were a member of an occupational scheme, where your employer may shoulder by far the greater proportion of the cost. Most employees in occupational pension schemes pay around five per cent of their earnings into a company pension scheme, when the real cost might well be around 25 per cent. Your employer may be willing to contribute towards your personal pension, although this is rare.

- Defined contribution rather than defined benefit – personal pensions are all money purchase; what you pay for is what you get. What the accumulated cash sum will buy at retirement age in terms of benefits may bear no relation to your earnings at that time. More than nine out of ten occupational schemes pay benefits linked to your final salary on retirement, and many funds pay increases to pensioners in retirement.

- No guaranteed life assurance – an occupational pension scheme will generally pay three or four times your annual salary as a tax-free lump sum if you die before retirement. You may not be able to obtain life cover through your personal pension, and more importantly, you'll have to pay it yourself.

Job changers

Very few people work for just one employer all their working life, and changing jobs will affect your pension entitlement.

For example, most occupational pension schemes offer a proportion of your salary at retirement – usually one-sixtieth – for every year of service. If you were retiring today on a salary of £25,000 after having worked for the same employer for forty years, you would collect a pension of 40/60ths of £25,000 – ie £16,666. If you had been with the same employer for only 20 years, the pension would be 20/60th of £25,000 – ie £8,333. In a good scheme, once you started to draw this pension it would be increased from time to time to take account of inflation, although currently there is no legal requirement on the employer to do so. Employees in public sector schemes enjoy full inflation proofing of benefits.

But if you change jobs, the situation is very different. Before 1978, if you changed jobs you would generally find that your pension benefits would be frozen within the scheme. You might, for example, have been with your employer for five years, in which case you would have earned 5/60ths – but not based on your salary at retirement age. It would be 5/60th of your salary at the date you left and there was, and still is, no legal requirement to uprate this to take account of inflation.

Since 1985, part of your pension benefits earned after that date, and left with your former employer on changing jobs, have to be given a degree of inflation proofing. They must be uprated in line with inflation or five per cent, whichever is the smaller figure. This has recently been improved by legislation and now all of your benefits earned will have to be increased.

For example, if you left your company scheme in 1990 after five years service and your salary at the date of leaving was £15,000, then your pension entitlement would be 5/60th of £15,000 – ie £1,250. If you leave this pension with your former employer, it must be uprated by the lesser of inflation or five per cent.

Clearly, you will reach retirement age with a pension which has lost its buying power if inflation runs at a higher rate.

If you have been in a company pension scheme between 1978 (when SERPS started) and today, a proportion of your frozen pension known as the Guaranteed Minimum Pension (GMP) has to be uprated each year in line with wage inflation. The GMP is similar to the pension you would have earned if you had been contracted into SERPS. (Most occupational pension schemes are contracted out of SERPS.) Pension benefits earned prior to 1978 are not protected by law against inflation, although a good employer may be prepared to offer some voluntary inflation proofing.

It is clear that young women becoming members of an occupational scheme today will have a substantial measure of inflation proofing for their pensions, even if they do change jobs. Older employees, particularly those with a considerable number of years of service prior to 1978, will have lost a large proportion of the benefits earned if they have changed jobs.

To summarize, pension entitlement earned before 1978 is not protected against inflation at all – although a good company scheme might voluntarily offer some uprating. Pension entitlement earned since 1978 will have a degree of inflation proofing – the Guaranteed Minimum Pension (GMP), which is the pension you would have earned if you had stayed in SERPS, is uprated in line with wage inflation.

Pension benefits earned since 1985 in excess of the GMP will be uprated by the lesser of inflation or five per cent, whichever is the less, and since January 1990, anyone leaving a final salary scheme will also have their benefits above the GMP earned before the 1985 revaluation.

Clearly, it would be wise to make good any shortfall by making contributions to an AVC or FSAVC scheme or by saving in some other way.

What are the options?

When you leave a job, you will have several options. If you have been in the company pension scheme for less than two years, the scheme does not have to offer you any preserved benefits, but most schemes now do. This is because the cost of administering a very small frozen pension would be high. Instead, you could be given back the contributions you have made. There will be two deductions made from this sum: the first is to buy you back into SERPS (assuming that the company scheme was contracted out), and the second is a deduction of 10 per cent of the balance to take account of the tax relief you have already had on the contributions.

– Preserved pensions

If you change jobs after two years' service, your former employer must offer you preserved pension rights and the right to transfer your benefits if you wish. You can, however, claim back all contributions paid by you prior to 1975. Whether it is to your advantage to do so will depend on your employer's policy on uprating pension rights to take account of inflation. If you have a money purchase scheme, this will not apply – the value of your 'pot' will grow with the underlying investment performance.

Indeed, for high earners where a considerable proportion of the pension rights earned are pre-1978, before SERPS was introduced and either not protected by inflation at all, or since 1985 only up to a maximum of five per cent, it is vital to know whether your former employer intends to uprate these benefits because it will affect your decision on whether to opt for a preserved pension or go elsewhere.

– *A transfer payment to your new employer's scheme*

Your former employer is obliged to offer you a transfer value for your pension rights, but your new employer is not obliged to take that transfer. Even if he is prepared to do so, the amount of pension it buys is unlikely to be the same as the pension you would have enjoyed if you left it with your former employer; it might be better or worse.

There are many reasons for this: your former employer may be mean or generous in the way he calculates the present-day value of your preserved pension benefits (although there are guidelines for calculating some of the benefits); the value of the mandatory and promised increases must be included in the calculation, although the value of any discretionary uprating need not be, and the transfer sum, if accepted by your new employer, may buy better or worse benefits because of the structure of his scheme.

One thing is certain: because of the way transfer values are calculated, you will get a larger sum at a time when interest rates are low. If you change jobs when interest rates are high, it will pay you to defer taking a transfer until rates come down.

A good company scheme will offer you independent advice on whether to take a transfer payment or opt for preserved pension benefits. The decision on whether to transfer is difficult and will vary from scheme to scheme.

– *Transfer to a personal pension*

If you prefer, you can take your transfer sum and put it into a personal pension, chosen by yourself. Here again, whether this is better than opting for preserved benefits with your former employer or putting the money into the scheme run by your new employer will depend on a number of factors – your former employer's policy on uprating deferred pension benefits, your new employer's policy on crediting you with pension years of service, and the likely benefits you will earn with a personal pension. Like all decisions on personal pensions, the benefits earned will depend very much on the investment performance of the fund in which your personal pension contributions are invested. You will need to take professional advice.

You should also bear in mind that a high proportion of complaints to the Occupational Pensions Advisory Service (OPAS) concern the difficulty pensioners have in tracing pensions earned with former employers and getting the firm to pay up.

Over the course of your working life, firms you have worked for may be taken over, pension funds merged and benefits policy altered. It is not unknown for employers to lose track of what happened to deferred pension benefits earned 20 years ago, so taking your transfer sum and putting it in a personal pension may be the easiest way of keeping tabs on what has happened to your pension.

For employees who are not in a final salary scheme but in a money purchase pension plan, the decision is easier. Money purchase pension schemes do not have benefits linked to your final salary. Your contributions and any made by the employer are invested to produce a fund at retirement which is then used to buy an annuity or income for life. This is exactly the same as a personal pension, so the decision to transfer or stay will depend on how the investment performance of the company scheme compares with the investment performance of the best personal pension policies. If it is poor, take the cash transfer value and put it into a personal pension.

Non-earning women

If you have no earned income, you are not eligible to make contributions to a pension scheme of any sort. If you are married or have a partner on whom you rely financially, you should find out what provision is being made for you and any children there may be.

If your husband is in a good company scheme, you could expect to receive a lump sum of three or four times his gross earnings, should he die before retirement age. You should also be entitled to a widow's and dependant's pension of up to two-thirds of your spouse's pension if he dies either before or after retirement. If, however, you get divorced, you may lose your entitlement to any of these benefits.

If you are not married, your partner may be able to make arrangements for these benefits to be paid to you. But if he has a former wife, technically she will be entitled to any pension benefits. Some company pension trustees use their discretion and either split the benefits between both claimants, or pay both claimants anything between a half to the full widow's pension.

If your partner or spouse is not a member of an occupational pension scheme, you should ask what pension provision he has made. At the very least, make sure he has life assurance which will provide a sensible lump sum of at least four times his income, should he die.

Having checked on the provision made by your spouse or partner, your only alternative course of action if you have no earnings is to save in something like a Personal Equity Plan or other long-term saving scheme.

This is also a useful alternative investment for those high-earning individuals who come up against the 'earnings cap' for pension tax relief. See Chapter 2 on Savings, page 39, for full details.

On reaching retirement

When you reach retirement age, you will generally be faced with a number of decisions. The first will be whether to commute part of the pension benefits and take a tax-free cash lump sum. The exact amount which you can take will depend on the pension mix. You may have deferred benefits from a number of occupational schemes, benefits from AVCs, benefits from personal pensions and self-employed retirement annuities, and the entitlement will vary on each.

Generally speaking, it pays to take the maximum lump sum – bearing in mind that there is then less money left to buy your pension, which will necessarily be lower. This gives you greater flexibility, but you will clearly need independent professional advice on how and where to invest this money.

You will probably also have the option to take a lower initial pension but have benefits index-linked to take account of inflation. The problem with this is that full index linking means that you will have to accept a cut of around 50 per cent in the pension you take initially. However, bear in mind that a pension of £20,000 a year may sound fine today if you have just retired on earnings of £30,000 a year. Ten years down the line, it is unlikely to be adequate.

Personal pension investors will also be offered the opportunity to take the accumulated fund at retirement age and shop around for the best annuity rate in order to maximise the pension income. This also has the advantage of offering you the opportunity to consolidate all your pension in one place, rather than collecting it from several different sources. You should take independent advice from a pensions consultant on where the best rates can be obtained.

Conclusion

The important point to remember about pension planning is that the sooner you start, the better. Pensions are a complicated field and you will undoubtedly need independent financial advice at different times throughout your working life.

ℬUYING A HOUSE

When it comes to buying a home, women are on exactly the same footing as male purchasers. If anything they are preferred by the lenders – indeed, single females are considered a particularly good risk. As one building society manager put it, 'Women owners tend to get married and then there are two salaries to back the loan. Single men tend to get married and acquire liabilities.'

The only difficulty women homebuyers are likely to encounter is that they do not, on average, earn as much as men, so they will not be able to borrow as much as the average male buyer. If you are divorced and your only income is maintenance payments from a former husband, you will generally need a guarantee from your former husband before the lender will grant a mortgage. A parent, or other friend or relative can also provide the guarantee but they should understand that in the event of your not being able to make the repayments – perhaps because your former husband is in arrears with maintenance – they will be liable for the loan.

The average female homebuyer, however, is generally in exactly the same position as her male counterpart. It has been said very many times before that buying a house is the biggest single purchase you will ever make and is therefore worth getting right.

What few people ever tell you is that it can be the most exciting and rewarding thing you will ever do – or the most disappointing and frustrating event of your life.

In 1990, 775,000 homebuyers raised a building society loan* to buy a house and more than half of them were first-time buyers. Very few people can afford to buy for cash and first-time buyers often

* The expressions 'loan' and 'mortgage' are used interchangeably throughout this chapter.

Regional house prices – average house prices and annual percentage change, 1990/91 July to July

	Price £	Change %
Greater London	88,000	-4
South East	80,000	-5
South West	65,000	-4
East Anglia	59,000	-4
East Midlands	56,000	-2
West Midlands	62,000	0
Yorks/Humberside	55,000	+1
North West	57,000	+5
North of England	50,000	+3
Wales	50,000	-2
Scotland	57,000	+6
Northern Ireland	37,000	+12

Figures to 1.7.91

Source: Halifax Building Society

need to borrow anything up to 100 per cent of the purchase price.

To give you some idea of what to expect, in 1990 the average first-time buyer in the UK needed an 83 per cent loan and borrowed £36,807 to buy a house or flat costing £44,148. This compares with former owners who paid £75,581 for their new home, borrowing 59.1 per cent of the purchase price – a loan of £44,638.

There are also wide regional variations in house prices so if you are thinking of coming to London to work, or you have to move from, say, Liverpool to Bristol, you will need to know roughly what you will have to pay for a property.

ARRANGING THE FINANCE

How much can I borrow?

If you want to avoid disappointment, the first thing you must establish is the amount you can borrow. Buying a house is just like everything else; once you start looking, you will inevitably discover that the house you fall in love with costs more than you can afford.

With increased competition among lenders it is easier to borrow now than ever before and banks and building societies are prepared to make loans that may be larger than you can afford. Make sure you do not overstretch yourself.

Work out a budget, taking into account all your current outgoings on everything from existing loan repayments, gas, electricity, telephone and the like to food, clothing and holidays.

Be realistic about what you can sensibly afford to spend on mortgage repayments.

Most lenders use a formula for establishing the maximum amount you can borrow. For the employed person it is usually three, occasionally three and a half, times your gross earnings (your salary before any deductions are made for tax, National Insurance contributions or pensions).

If you earn bonuses or commission, generally speaking, only a

---

Budget Check List

1. Rent or mortgage repayments
2. Council Tax
3. Electricity
4. Gas, Water
5. Telephone
6. House insurance
7. Car running costs and petrol
8. HP, personal loan or credit card repayments
9. Personal insurance
10. Life assurance and/or savings schemes
11. Travel
12. Food
13. Clothes
14. Holidays
15. Miscellaneous

proportion of this will be taken into account, unless there is a guaranteed amount.

For example, if your gross earnings are £15,000 a year you will be able to borrow, typically, £45,000, with some lenders advancing up to £52,500.

If you are buying with a friend, relative, partner, or spouse, the formula is usually three times the larger salary plus the smaller income. A couple where the husband earns £25,000 and the wife £10,000 will be able to borrow up to £85,000. Some lenders use the formula of two and a half times the joint earnings which produces a very similar maximum loan.

The temptation will be to borrow up to the limit but this can be dangerous. If you work in a cyclical industry where lay-offs are common you could find yourself out of work. Even the professions such as accountancy, medicine and the law are no longer immune from redundancies.

Take into account also that there will be considerable costs associated with buying a house or moving, such as stamp duty, legal and survey fees, not to mention new carpets and curtains; most of these will have to be found in cash.

Self-employed homebuyers have a tougher time generally. The lender will want to see three years' audited accounts as proof of your earning capacity. Some will accept a letter of confirmation of your earnings from your accountant.

The alternative is to opt for a non-status loan. This means that you self-certify your earnings – the lender accepts your assurances on what you earn – but you will find that you are unlikely to be able to borrow more than 75 per cent of the purchase price. Most non-status loans are offered through mortgage brokers.

Many self-employed people find that their earnings fluctuate, so avoid the temptation to borrow a large amount after a good year.

Divorced or separated women, single mothers and those on maternity leave or working part time will all have difficulty in obtaining a loan, not because of status, but simply because their earnings are likely to be low and irregular, if they have any earnings at all. Some lenders will treat maintenance payments from a former husband as 'income' but will generally require a guarantee from the payer.

Where should I go for a loan?

For the average borrower, whether you are a first-time buyer or have bought before, your local building society branch is as good a place to start as any. There are now a wide variety of loans on offer, and all lenders have to be competitive and cannot afford to be out of line in terms of the range of products offered or interest rates and are likely to be competitive. The large lenders also have wide experience of lending and are less likely to encourage you to take out a loan that is unsuitable or one you cannot really afford. In short, they are likely to be more conservative than some of the other lenders.

The centralised lenders which operate mostly through mortgage brokers and other intermediaries often offer attractive terms to new borrowers, but their rate may not remain competitive.

The cost of moving a loan or remortgaging can be considerable. Large lenders like the high street banks and building societies are under enormous pressure to keep their terms competitive and they cannot afford to charge more than the going rate.

However, there is a huge variety of loans on offer and not all of them are available from the large lenders.

If you are keen to buy a house of unusual construction, want a loan that is in some way different from the norm or want to remortgage an existing property, it will pay to consult a reputable mortgage broker.

This is easier said than done, since there are still some unscrupulous loan sharks around. The worst offenders are prepared to arrange mortgages for people who really cannot afford one, at extortionate interest rates of anything up to 70 per cent or more.

A reputable mortgage broker will usually be a member of one of the Self Regulatory Organisations (SROs) set up under the Financial Services Act 1986. A broker cannot give advice on investment products linked to the home loan without being a member of an SRO.

Check whether the mortgage broker you consult is a member of either FIMBRA (The Financial Intermediaries Managers and Brokers Regulatory Association) or IMRO (The Investment Managers Regulatory Organisation). You would be well advised not to use an intermediary who is not a member of either of these organisations, even if he is a licensed credit broker.

There are plenty of other people around who will be only too glad to give you advice on your loan – estate agents, the bank or building society manager, or life assurance salesmen. These people are not able to give genuinely independent, impartial advice because they are the tied agents of a financial institution. All they can offer are the products sold by their particular institution. If you want genuinely impartial advice, go to an intermediary who is a member of FIMBRA or IMRO.

WHAT WILL MY LOAN COST?

Term

Most new home loans are for twenty-five years or thirty years and are designed to be repaid at retirement age. If you are, say, already in your fifties, the lender may insist that the term of the loan is shorter. For example, a borrower of 52 might be offered a thirteen- or fifteen-year loan. The shorter the term of the loan, the higher the monthly repayments will be. For example, the monthly cost of a twenty-five-year repayment loan of £45,000 at 11.95 per cent is £412.35 after tax relief. The same loan over a fifteen-year period works out at £492.45 a month.

Monthly cost of a £30,000 home loan over varying periods – mortgage rate 11.95%

Term of Loan in Years	Monthly Cost Tax Relief 25% £
5	642.00
10	388.00
15	309.30
20	273.00
25	253.50
30	242.40

Source: The Building Societies Association

Most loans granted today are linked to life or pensions products. You pay interest only on the loan, which is eventually paid off at the end of the term from the cash sum accumulated in the life or pensions policy. In this case, the interest payments on the mortgage will be the same, regardless of the term of the loan. However, the monthly premium on the savings type life or pensions policy will generally be higher if the term of the loan is short, because the money paid into the scheme has had less time to accumulate and generate profits. You may already have existing policies which have been in force for some time, and which are acceptable to the lender, in which case this should help to keep the cost down.

Interest rates

Clearly, the other factor which will affect the cost of your loan is the interest rate charged. Make sure you know the APR (Annual Percentage Rate). The APR is a formula which describes the interest rate on the total cost of credit.

The advantage of using the APR is that all loans quoting an interest rate as an APR are comparable in terms of cost. Bank and building society loans of more than £15,000 are not subject to the APR and, as a result, a loan from one lender at a quoted interest rate of, say, 12

Monthly mortgage repayments net of basic rate tax on a 25 year loan*

Loan	11.95%
	£
£30,000	253.50
£40,000	359.40
£50,000	465.30
£60,000	571.20
£70,000	677.10
£80,000	783.00
£90,000	888.90
£100,000	994.80

* Repayments have been calculated using the Constant Net Repayment method. This means that tax relief will stay constant throughout the term of the loan.

Source: The Building Societies Association

per cent may be more expensive than a loan from another at the same quoted rate. This is due to many factors, but most commonly because one lender charging 12 per cent compounds the interest on the annual basis, another on a monthly basis and a third daily.

The only accurate way to compare the cost is, therefore, to look at the monthly payments. The table on page 100 gives you some idea of what a straight repayment loan might cost.

WHAT TYPE OF LOAN?

Time was when the choice of loan was limited to a straight repayment loan or one linked to a life policy. Today, competition amongst lenders is so fierce that a wide array of loans, each with different terms and conditions, is now available.

It is important to make sure you have the loan most suited to your circumstances and that you understand how it works. Some types of loans – in particular, deferred interest schemes or currency loans – have some potentially dangerous consequences if you don't understand what you are taking on.

Whatever the fancy terms of a loan, there are two basic ways of repaying a mortgage – by straight repayments, where you gradually pay off the sum borrowed over the agreed term, or an interest-only mortgage, where the original sum borrowed is repaid from the proceeds of an associated investment scheme.

This is most commonly a life or pensions policy but increasingly, lenders are prepared to accept unit or investment trust regular savings schemes, or Personal Equity Plans (PEPs) as the investment vehicle to repay the loan.

Straight repayment or annuity loan

Repayment loans are suitable for all borrowers and are generally among the cheapest on offer.

Years ago, this was the only type of loan available. Monthly repayments consist of part capital (the original sum borrowed) and part interest. By the end of the agreed term of the loan – usually twenty-five or thirty years – the capital is fully repaid, the mortgage is discharged and you own your home outright.

Most lenders recommend that you take out a mortgage protection policy to run alongside the repayment loan. This will provide a lump sum sufficient to repay the outstanding debt should you die before the loan matures. It does not provide any additional benefits.

Years ago, this was the only type of loan in existence; now, a much wider variety of loans is available.

Endowment or pension-linked loans – interest only

The vast majority of mortgages are now granted on an endowment or pension-linked basis. With this type of loan you make no repayment of the capital; interest only is paid throughout the term. Alongside runs a savings type life or pensions policy (or sometimes a combination of the two) which matures at the same time as the loan, the proceeds of which are used to pay off the loan at the end of the term.

With both endowment and pension-linked loans there are extra benefits, the actual amount of which will depend on the investment track record of the life assurance company.

The endowment policy provides a sum of money which should repay the loan when it matures and provide a tax-free, cash lump sum as a bonus.

The pension policy also provides cash to repay the mortgage, but there is an annual pension which is paid in addition at retirement age.

Personal pension policies allow you to take a cash lump sum at retirement in return for a lower pension and it is this money which is used to repay the home loan. You are also entitled to tax relief on the pension premiums at your highest rate paid.

Only those borrowers eligible to take out a personal pension – the self-employed and employees who are not members of an occupational pension scheme – can qualify for a pension-linked loan, although in certain circumstances, members of a company pension scheme can also qualify.

The table overleaf shows the relative costs and benefits of endowment, pension, and repayment loans at varying rates of tax.

There is nothing magical about using a life or pensions policy as the investment vehicle to repay the loan. It is simply a means of saving. Pension policies do have the advantage of tax relief on the contributions, but you have to weigh this against the higher cost and lack of flexibility of a pension-linked loan.

Comparative costs of various mortgage repayment methods

Monthly cost of a 25-year, £30,000 mortgage for a single woman aged 28, net of 25% tax relief - mortgage rate 11.95%			
Monthly Cost	Repayment	Endowment	Pension
	£	£	£
Interest	456.85	423.23	423.23
Life/Pension Premium	5.00	61.20	116.11*
Total	461.85	484.43	539.34
Residual Benefits**	None	15,400	12,500 plus 18,800 p/a pension

NOTE
* *Combined life and pension premium net of 25 per cent tax relief.*
** *These are estimated benefits after repayment of £50,000 loan and assuming an investment return over the 25-year term of 10.5 per cent on the endowment and 13 per cent on the pension fund.*
Source: Norwich Union

An increasing number of lenders are prepared to accept unit trust or investment trust regular savings schemes as the investment vehicle which is used to repay the loan. This is a far more efficient means of saving because the charges on these schemes are much lower than on a life or pensions policy and the schemes are more flexible with no surrender penalties if you want to cash in early.

In addition, if your regular saving scheme is organised within a PEP (Personal Equity Plan), the income generated by the underlying investments is tax free and the proceeds when you cash in are free from capital gains tax (CGT).

Whatever investment vehicle you use to repay your home loan, there are basically two different types – endowment or unit linked. Turn to the chapter on savings on page 39 for a full description of the differences between the two.

Fixed rate loan

Most mortgages have a variable interest rate which fluctuates in line with the bank base rate. The table below shows just how volatile mortgage rates can be and how widely they can vary in a relatively short space of time.

A fixed rate loan should never be confused with a fixed repayment loan, which is a very different animal. The interest rate on a fixed rate loan does not vary but remains constant, usually for a period of anything between one and five years. There have occasionally been fixed rate loans on offer for longer terms.

The advantage of a fixed rate loan is that the monthly repayments remain the same during the fixed rate period and you know precisely what your outgoings will be – very useful if you have borrowed heavily and would be badly hit by an increase in the home loan rate. Many homebuyers who borrowed in early 1988, when mortgages stood at 9.8 per cent, found themselves in severe difficulties by early 1990 when the mortgage rate shot up to 15.4 per cent.

Clearly, it is not the best time to enter into a fixed rate loan when interest rates are high. Bear in mind, however, that the average mortgage interest rate paid by homebuyers over the past ten to fifteen years has been around 12 per cent, so any fixed rate loan at around that level is a reasonable deal.

The advantage of a fixed rate loan is that if you have signed for a loan at, say, 12.5 per cent for three years and interest rates move to 15.0 per cent, you are saving money. But of course the reverse is true if interest rates fall during the period. For most people, particularly those with large loans, the security of knowing exactly what your outgoings will be is worth the risk that interest rates might fall during the fixed rate term.

One word of warning: fixed rate loans invariably have penalties for early redemption of the mortgage during the fixed rate term – typically, three to six months' interest. You are effectively locked into the loan during the fixed rate period.

Fixed rate loans can be straight repayment mortgages or interest-only and linked to a life or pensions policy.

Cap and collar

An alternative to fixed rate loans which gives you the best of both worlds is a 'cap and collar' loan. This limits the amount by which the mortgage interest rate can vary – either up or down. For example, you may

Mortgage rate changes over the past twenty years

Date of Change	Rate
1969 (March)	8.5
1971 (October)	8.0
1972 (September)	8.5
1973 (April)	9.5
1973 (Aug)	10.0
1973 (Sept)	11.0
1976 (April)	10.5
1976 (October)	12.25
1977 (April)	11.25
1977 (June)	10.5
1977 (Sept)	9.5
1978 (Jan)	8.5
1978 (June)	9.75
1978 (Nov)	11.75
1979 (July)	12.5
1980 (December)	14.0
1981 (March)	13.0
1981 (October)	15.0
1982 (March)	13.5
1982 (Aug)	12.0
1982 (Nov)	10.0
1983 (June)	11.25
1984 (March)	10.25
1984 (July)	12.5
1984 (Nov)	11.75
1985 (Jan)	12.75
1985 (March)	13.75
1985 (Aug)	12.75
1986 (March)	12.0
1986 (June)	11.0
1986 (Nov)	12.25
1987 (May)	11.25
1988 (Jan)	10.0
1988 (May)	9.5
1988 (Aug)	11.5
1988 (Oct)	12.75
1989 (Jan)	13.5
1990 (Feb)	14.5
1990 (April)	15.4
1990 (October)	14.5
1991 (Feb)	14.5
1991 (May)	12.95

Source: The Building Societies Association

borrow at 12 per cent but the loan has a 14 per cent 'cap' and a 10 per cent 'collar'. This means that whatever mortgage rates do generally, your interest rate will not rise above 14 per cent or fall below 10 per cent. Some home loans have a cap only and no collar.

There is usually a fee for this facility, which is often added to the amount borrowed. Alternatively, the interest rate charged initially may be slightly higher than the standard rate. For example, you may have a mortgage capped at 15.0 per cent and pay 12.5 per cent for this facility when the going rate is generally 12.0 per cent.

Both cap and collar loans and fixed rate mortgages tend to be available through mortgage brokers, although lenders do sometimes offer them direct.

When interest rates are low, fixed rate loans and capped loans tend to be snapped up very fast. Anyone thinking of remortgaging should get all their paperwork ready so that as soon as the fixed rate money becomes available, you are ready to go ahead.

Cap and collar loans can be straight repayment mortgages or interest-only and linked to a life or pensions policy.

Fixed repayment loans

Do not confuse this with a fixed rate loan – it is very different. With a fixed repayment mortgage, your monthly payments remain constant throughout an agreed term, usually one to five years. But the actual interest rate charged will vary in line with interest rates generally.

You may, for example, agree to fix your repayments at 12 per cent for three years. During that period, the mortgage rate might rise to, say 14 per cent and fall to 11 per cent. You continue to make the same level of repayments as though the mortgage rate had remained at 12 per cent. But any unpaid interest at the end of the fixed repayment period is added to the sum originally borrowed.

Provided you choose a level of repayment which is sensible and realistic, say, 11 or 12 per cent, the situation will probably even itself out over a five-year period. There will be times when your fixed repayments are higher than necessary and other times when they will be lower than is required.

Nevertheless, there is a potential danger for homebuyers who borrow a high proportion of the purchase price of a property – say, 95 per cent – in a dull or falling house price market. If the fixed repayments are at a rate lower than the actual rate charged, the debt will increase and you could find yourself with a loan which is bigger than the value of the property and you will be unable to move house.

Fixed repayment loans can be either straight repayment mortgages or interest-only and linked to a life or pension policy. They are suitable for anyone who needs to know precisely what their outgoings will be, and cannot afford to see an increase in monthly payments.

Deferred interest mortgages

This type of loan should be treated with caution. Part of the interest charged is deferred, rolled up, and added to the original loan at a later date. Your debt increases and at some stage, usually three to five years later, you will have to start making repayments on a larger sum.

You may, for example take out a £50,000 loan at 12 per cent and agree to defer three per cent of the interest in the first year, two per cent in the second and one per cent in the third. At the end of the third year, you will have £3,000 of unpaid interest which is added to the loan and you must make repayments on the larger sum.

The danger is that you may not be able to afford the higher repayments in three years' time. But more alarming is the possibility, if you have borrowed a high proportion of the purchase price, that the loan will be larger than the value of the house.

Deferred interest or low start schemes, as they are sometimes called, are suitable only for those homebuyers who are certain that their earnings will increase; articled clerks, for example, or trainees in a stable profession.

Deferred interest mortgages can be either repayment or interest-only linked to a life or pensions policy.

Currency loans

These have received a lot of publicity in recent years, but are not suitable for the average homebuyer. In its simplest form, the currency loan is a facility to borrow in another currency and make repayments in that currency.

The advantage is that interest rates in other currencies are frequently considerably below the mortgage rate charged in the UK; the disadvantage is that if the currency in which you borrow strengthens against the pound, your debt will increase. Of course, the reverse is true.

For example, if you borrow £100,000 in Swiss francs at an exchange rate of SF2.64 to the pound and the Swiss franc weakens to SF2.83 to the pound, your original £100,000 loan is reduced to £93,286 in sterling terms. But the reverse could have happened. Had the Swiss franc strengthened against the pound to SF2.30, your debt would have increased to £114,782. You would have had the advantage of a lower interest rate of around 8 per cent but this may not be sufficient to compensate for the increase in debt. Low interest rates generally go hand in hand with a strong currency.

However, there are currency mortgages on offer where the currency in which your loan is denominated is chosen by professional foreign exchange experts who switch from one currency to another to obtain both an interest rate advantage and protection of the capital sum borrowed. With some managed schemes, the loan is switched into a basket of currencies to limit the risk, but the interest rate advantage is also reduced.

In short, you should only take out a currency loan if you can afford to carry the risk of the currency moving against you. This type of loan is only for the sophisticated homebuyer wanting to borrow £100,000 or more.

Mortgage discounts
Many lenders offer discounts to certain homebuyers – typically, 1 per cent for the first year. Generally, first-time buyers and those who want larger than average loans can benefit from these discounts.

Low start mortgages
These come in a variety of forms ranging from a deferred interest scheme (see above) to variations which use some of your deposit to subsidise repayments during the early months of the loan.

Low start schemes should not be confused with low cost endowment mortgages which are simply straight endowment-linked home loans where the life assurance premium is kept to a minimum.

TAX RELIEF

Monthly payments on your loan are reduced considerably because you are entitled to tax relief on the interest on the first £30,000 of a mortgage. This is given at the basic rate of tax paid on any mortgage used to buy your 'principal private residence'. Generally speaking, this is the house in which you live, although if you have more than one house you can opt to have one or the other designated your principal private residence.

This is important, because your principal private residence is also free from capital gains tax (CGT) on any profit you make when you sell.

If, for example, you buy a house for £50,000 and sell it three years later for £57,000, there will be no CGT on the £7,000 profit if the house is your principal private residence.

If the house was a holiday or weekend cottage, you would be potentially liable for CGT at either 25 per cent or 40 per cent (depending on the rate of income tax you pay) on the full £7,000 profit, which works out at £2,800 for a 40 per cent taxpayer, £1,750 for the basic rate taxpayer.

You probably would not pay the whole amount, however, unless you have made profits in the same tax year on, say, selling shares. The first £5,500 of gains in the 1991-92 tax year is free from CGT. For a married couple who own a second home jointly, this means the first £11,000 of profit is effectively tax free.

For the average borrower, however, with only one home, the main advantage of the tax relief is that it reduces the payments on the mortgage on the first £30,000 borrowed.

The table overleaf shows the monthly cost for each £1,000 borrowed over 25 years with tax relief at 25 per cent and without tax relief (to illustrate the cost of each £1,000 borrowed over the £30,000 cut-off point for mortgage interest relief).

All borrowers are entitled to tax relief, regardless of whether or not they pay tax, which means that every borrower makes the lower payments on the first £30,000. Most borrowers will be granted the tax relief automatically under MIRAS (Mortgage Interest Relief at Source) when they make their monthly payments.

When you are granted your mortgage, the lender will ask you to fill in a form, Miras 70 or Miras 3, which will ensure that you are

Mortgage cost per month for each £1,000 borrowed over 25 years – repayment loan

Interest Rate	With 25% Tax Relief	Without Tax Relief
	£	£
10.0	7.45	9.19
10.25	7.61	9.36
10.5	7.71	9.54
10.75	7.84	9.72
11.0	7.98	9.90
11.25	8.11	10.08
11.5	8.22	10.26
11.75	8.35	10.45
12.0	8.49	10.63
12.25	8.63	10.81
12.5	8.77	11.0
12.75	8.87	11.19
13.0	9.01	11.37
13.25	9.15	11.56
13.5	9.26	11.75
13.75	9.40	11.94
14.0	9.54	12.13
14.25	9.68	12.32
14.5	9.83	12.51
14.75	9.94	12.70
15.0	10.08	12.90
15.25	10.23	13.09
15.5	10.34	13.82
15.75	10.48	13.48
16.0	10.63	13.67
16.25	10.78	13.87
16.5	10.89	14.06
16.75	11.07	14.26
17.0	11.19	14.46

Repayments have been calculated according to the Constant Net Repayment method. This means that tax relief will stay constant throughout the term of the loan. The alternative is an annually reviewed loan which will result in lower initial repayments, rising as the tax relief in each monthly payment diminishes.

Source: The Building Societies Association

automatically given mortgage interest relief. You can alternatively get the relief as a tax rebate at the end of the tax year when you file your tax return.

The majority of loans currently being granted are linked to a life or pensions policy, in which case the payments made to the lender consist of interest only; there is no repayment of the amount borrowed until the life or pensions policies mature, when the proceeds are used to pay off the loan. Tax relief on the interest payments will therefore remain constant throughout the term of the loan.

With a pension-linked loan, tax relief is also granted at the current basic rate of 25 per cent paid on the premiums for the pension policy. Higher rate taxpayers can claim the extra 15 per cent relief through their code number or as a tax rebate at the end of the year. There is no tax relief on life policy premiums; it was abolished for policies taken out after 13 March 1984.

It is worth mentioning here that if you have policies signed before that date on which tax relief is still available, it is generally worth hanging on to them unless the life assurance company has a very bad investment track record. Some lenders, salesmen or intermediaries, may try to persuade you to cancel them and take out new policies. If in any doubt about what to do, consult an independent financial adviser who is a member of FIMBRA or IMRO. See the Appendix for details of these and other related organisations.

Borrowers with a straight repayment, or annuity loan as it is called, may find that their monthly repayments go up – albeit very slightly – every year, even when there has been no change in the mortgage rate. This is usually because with a straight repayment loan you have a choice of the way the mortgage interest relief is calculated – 'annual review' or 'constant net repayments'.

Each monthly repayment consists of part interest and part repayment of the capital. With a constant net repayment loan, the tax relief is evened out over the term of the loan and remains, as its name suggests, constant.

With an annually reviewed loan you receive the actual tax relief to which you are entitled. This will go down during the term of the loan as the capital repayment element of each monthly payment increases. As the capital is repaid, so the interest charge diminishes and with it the tax relief. Most lenders give you a choice of either constant net repayments or annually reviewed repayments. The latter is the better bet for buyers who expect to move house again within three or four years.

BUYING COSTS

Arrangement fees

With your finance arranged, you can now start looking for your new home. This is when the additional costs start to mount up. The first expense may be the mortgage arrangement fee.

You will generally not be charged an arrangement fee unless you use a mortgage broker or other intermediary. The fee may be a flat charge of anything between £100 and £500, or a percentage of the amount advanced – anything between 0.5 per cent and 1 per cent. The arrangement fee is often negotiable, but you should sort this out with the intermediary at the start. It is not usual for the intermediary to charge an arrangement fee if you are also taking out new life or pensions policies on which he will earn commission.

Lenders sometimes charge an arrangement fee, particularly the centralised lenders, and some banks and building societies will charge a fee if the loan is a special offer like a fixed rate loan. This is generally no more than £50 to £100.

Some lenders will issue a mortgage certificate once the loan has been arranged to smooth the way when making an offer on a property. It confirms that you have a loan available.

Valuation fees

The lender will want a valuation of the property before making an offer of a mortgage. This is to ensure that the property is worth the seller's asking price and that the lender has adequate security for the loan.

The cost of the valuation will vary from lender to lender, and will depend on whether you decide to pay extra and have the more detailed inspection, called a Homebuyer's Report, or opt for a full structural survey.

The table shows valuation fees charged by the Halifax Building Society for a straight valuation and for a Homebuyer's Report. The fees

Cost of valuation or home buyer's report – Basic valuation

Purchase Price Not Exceeding £000	Gross £
25	85
50	105
75	125
100	145
150	175
200	205
250	235
300	265
350	295
400	330
450	360
500	390
Exceeding 500	By Arrangement

Source: Halifax Building Society

you pay are based on the asking price of the property, not the valuation price or the price you end up paying.

The valuation which is required by the lender says nothing about the condition of the property; it could be falling down or suffering from subsidence. It is simply a judgement on whether the property is worth the asking price. In the event that you are unable to make the mortgage repayments, the lender wants to be certain that the property can be sold for enough money to cover the loan.

Most valuations are for a figure something below the asking price and the lender will base the maximum advance on the lower valuation price. This can create difficulties if you need to borrow a high proportion of the purchase price. For example, you may need a 95 per cent loan on a property being sold for £50,000 – a mortgage of £47,500. The valuer says that the house is worth only £48,000, so the lender will reduce the maximum advance to £45,600, leaving you £1,900 short which you will have to find from other sources.

This is not a problem if you need a lower percentage loan of, say, 60 per cent or £30,000 on a £50,000 house. If the house is valued at £48,000, the lender will simply ask how much you want to borrow and will generally be prepared to advance up to 95 per cent of the valuation, provided you have sufficient income to support the repayments.

Do not rely on a simple valuation to tell you the structural state of the property, unless it is a new house or it is still under the builder's guarantee and is protected by a National House Building Council warranty. This gives you some protection for up to ten years in the event that serious structural faults are found. The owner must complain to the builder within the first two years of discovery of any structural defects and the builder is obliged to put them right at his own expense. In the event that the builder has gone out of business – a more common occurrence than you might think – you should complain direct to the NHBC.

Most lenders offer you the option of a Homebuyer's Report if you are prepared to pay extra. Alternatively, you can arrange a full structural

Cost of Homebuyer's Report

Purchase Price Not Exceeding *£000*	*Gross* *£*
50	200
75	250
100	300
150	350
200	400
250	450
300	500
350	550
400	600
450	650
500	700
Exceeding 500	By Arrangement

Source: The Halifax Building Society

survey which will give you a detailed review of the entire property.

A Homebuyer's Report is an important safeguard when you are buying older properties. It will generally cost around double the price of a valuation, but will include the valuation. It should identify anything seriously amiss with the house or flat such as subsidence, damp rot or woodworm in an obvious place like the cellar. The surveyor will usually make superficial checks of wiring and plumbing and the state of damp-proof courses, but he won't take up the floorboards to look at the joists, nor will he climb up onto the roof. If he is concerned that there might be something seriously wrong that he has been unable to check, he will tell you that a full structural survey is recommended.

A full structural survey may cost you more than a Homebuyer's Report, but with fierce competition for this area of business, you may be able to negotiate the full survey for not much more than the Homebuyer's Report.

Shop around and get quotes from several chartered surveyors before making a decision. In the past, the fee was a scale charge based on the value of the property. Some surveyors still try to impose the scale fees. This works against you if you are buying a property in an expensive area like central London. It takes no longer to survey a three-bedroomed house in Croydon than in the West Midlands, but the house prices will vary widely and the buyer in Croydon will pay more under the scale fee system than the buyer in the West Midlands.

A good surveyor will, however, base his fees on the size of the property and its construction. In a recent flat purchase, one buyer was quoted survey fees ranging from £250 to £850 for a two-bedroomed maisonette in central London. It pays to shop around.

Many estate agents are also chartered surveyors, or they will be able to recommend one in your area. It would be wise to use a chartered surveyor who is independent of the estate agent who is selling the property. Alternatively, the Royal Institution of Chartered Surveyors can give you the names of members operating near the property to be surveyed.

A full structural survey will review in considerable detail the condition of the property including plumbing, wiring, drainage, roofs, walls and damp-proof courses. The surveyor may recommend specialist investigations if problems like woodworm or dry rot emerge.

A good structural survey can be a useful negotiating tool when haggling over the price of a property. If the survey reveals that work costing, say, £5,000 is required to put the property in good order, you should be able to press for a reduction in price of at least that figure – possibly more if you take into account the inconvenience to you of having to get the work done.

If serious faults do emerge, the lender may well retain some of the mortgage advance until the necessary repair work is done, in which case you will probably need a bank bridging loan to cover the time when the repairs are being carried out. Do also take into account the traumas of moving into a new home and, possibly, having builders in the place for weeks or months.

Legal fees for conveyancing

Having found a property and made an offer (subject to contract and survey) you then ought to get the legal processes working. Here again, if you want to keep costs to a minimum it will pay to shop around. Solicitors compete fiercely for this business and all fees are negotiable.

Recent estimates for conveying a three-bedroomed house in Ealing, London, valued at £122,000, ranged from £350 to £1,200, and to find that one solicitor is charging as much as three or four times the estimate given by a competitor is quite commonplace. Whatever figure you eventually agree, make sure it is confirmed in writing.

You can sometimes save money by using the same solicitor as the lender, but not all lenders are happy to do this since they feel that there is a potential conflict of interest. You will have to pay for any work carried out by the lender's solicitor.

Making an offer does not finally commit you to buying the property, nor indeed does it guarantee that the seller won't accept another offer from another potential buyer. Only when you have exchanged contracts have you finally committed yourself to buying the property. (The law and practice are different in Scotland, as according to the Scottish practice, there is a binding contract immediately upon acceptance of the offer and therefore the offer is usually made at a later stage, after more detailed investigation.)

At this point you will probably be asked for a deposit which should be held as stakeholder by your solicitor. This may be anything from five to ten per cent of the value of the property and you will have to find this in cash before the mortgage is finally advanced, which will be on completion.

Some sellers will accept a deposit guarantee. This can be arranged through an insurance company or with your bank. The cost will depend on the amount of money involved and how creditworthy you are judged to be. Your solicitor should be able to give you details of how the insurance policy can be arranged. But if not, contact Legal and Professional Indemnity Ltd., P.O. Box 213, Tunbridge Wells, TN2 0LT, tel: (0892) 861234. The premium for a £5,000 deposit works out at £90.

Increasingly, in today's difficult property market, vendors, anxious to find a buyer, are prepared to exchange contracts without any deposit although they might request a 'comfort letter' from your bank, which simply states that you are creditworthy. The vendor might also request that the deposit you put down is released to him to use as a deposit on his purchase. It is unwise to agree to this, because there is a chance that you will have difficulty in getting this money back if things go wrong.

It is possible to do your own conveyancing or to use a cut-price specialist conveyancing firm. The Consumers' Association produces an action pack called *Do Your Own Conveyancing* (see Appendix for details; price £12.95, including post and packing) which is considered simple to use.

If you use a cut-price conveyancing firm, make sure it has adequate professional indemnity insurance so that you can sue if anything goes wrong.

Most homebuyers prefer the comfort of knowing that they are covered by the Law Society's compensation scheme should anything go amiss.

Other costs

The estimate your solicitor gives you will not include 'disbursements'. These include stamp duty which is levied at the rate of one per cent on all purchases of property over £30,000. It is payable on the total price, not just the excess over £30,000. For example, if you buy a property for £74,000 the stamp duty will be £740.

You will also have to pay land registry fees. These range from a

Land Registry fees

Value £		Fee £
0 –	20,000	30
20,001 –	25,000	35
25,001 –	30,000	40
30,001 –	35,000	45
35,001 –	40,000	55
40,001 –	45,000	65
45,001 –	50,000	75
50,001 –	60,000	90
60,001 –	70,000	110
70,001 –	80,000	130
80,001 –	90,000	150
90,001 –	100,000	180
100,001 –	200,000	220
200,001 –	300,000	260
300,001 –	400,000	300
400,001 –	600,000	350
600,001 –	800,000	400
800,001 –	1,000,000	450

Source: The Land Registry

minimum of £30 on property worth up to £20,000, to a maximum of £950 on property worth up £5 million or more. Fees on the average property costing between £100,000 and £200,000 work out at £220.

You will also have to set aside cash for removal costs – about £300 to £400 for the average three-bedroomed house, as well as money for carpets, curtains and the inevitable odds and ends such as plumbing in your kitchen equipment (if you are not buying this from the vendors).

The typical bill for buying a house will look something like the diagram on the next page:

Cost of buying a £120,000 house

*Broker's arrangement fee	£150
*Lender's fee	£80
Valuation fee – Homebuyer's Report	£350
Solicitor's fee	£400
Lender's solicitor's fee	£85
Land Registry fee	£220
Stamp duty	£1,200
Removal costs	£300
Building insurance	£215
TOTAL	£3,000

* *You may not be charged these fees.*

Step-by-step guide to buying a house

1 Consult lender or mortgage broker on the amount you can borrow.

2 Decide on type of loan. Ask lender to issue Mortgage Certificate.

3 Find suitable property within your price range.

4 Make offer subject to contract. If offer accepted, make formal application for the mortgage.

5 Arrange for survey or Homebuyer's Report to be carried out.

6 Find a solicitor or conveyancer and instruct him or her to start the legal processes.

*L*IFE ASSURANCE

Life assurance is a means of providing financially for your dependants in the event of your death. You pay a monthly or annual premium, and when you die, the insurance policy pays the guaranteed lump sum to a person named by you as the beneficiary, or to your estate. The most common variation on this is term assurance, which pays out only if you die during the term of the policy.

Women's life assurance needs are not very different from men's, although many non-working women greatly underestimate the value of their contribution to the running of the home and the cost of hiring childminders and replacement domestic help should they die while the children are young.

As a result, many couples insure the man's life, but forget how difficult life could be if the woman were to die, be seriously injured or be ill for any length of time.

Life assurance providing straight cover is essential for women. The mistake many people make is to confuse life assurance with savings policies. It is an understandable mistake, since the insurance industry sometimes blurs the distinctions.

Straight life assurance is about providing cash help for your dependants – children, spouse, partner or elderly relatives – if disaster strikes. The vast majority of policies sold are savings-type with profits endowments, or unit linked schemes, very often tied to the repayment of a home loan. If it's only life assurance that you require, make sure that this is what you're buying.

In today's competitive home loan market with profit margins under pressure, lenders are keen to promote life assurance-linked mortgages which earn them much higher commissions than on a straight repayment loan with a cheap term assurance.

This can be dangerous. Most home loan-linked endowment policies include enough life cover to pay off the mortgage, should you die before the end of the term, but it may be insufficient to provide for your dependants properly.

In the past, there was a reason for saving through a life policy – you generally received tax relief on the premiums. In 1984, this was abolished and with its removal went most of the reason for saving in this way. (Savings-type life policies are explained in Chapter 2 on page 57.)

Pure life assurance – the type which pays a lump sum or an income if you die or are unable to work through sickness or accident – is the only life assurance that everybody needs.

It is well worthwhile, therefore, understanding what the different types of life policy are used for and which is suited to your needs. The golden rule is to shop around yourself, or get independent advice. There are huge differences in the premiums quoted by the various life companies for exactly the same cover.

How much life assurance do I need?
Generally speaking, you need to insure your life for a minimum of three to four times your gross salary – more if you have a large mortgage which would eat up any cash from the insurance policy.

The exact amount will depend on individual circumstances. Much will depend on the income needed by any dependants – either spouse, partner, children or other relatives or friends.

It is arguable that a non-working wife without dependent children does not need life cover, since her spouse's standard of living will be largely unaffected by her death. However, your partner may become disabled and the cost of hiring household or nursing help, should you die before him, might be beyond his means.

Non-working wives with young children should insure their lives while the children are young for a sufficient amount to hire replacement domestic help, should they become ill or die unexpectedly.

If you have no dependants at the moment, you may not need life assurance. But the earlier you buy life cover, the cheaper it is and most people do acquire dependants at a later stage. It is better to overinsure than not to be able to afford proper cover. The older you are, the more expensive life assurance becomes.

For example, 15-year convertible term cover of £100,000 costs around £160 a year at age 29, but a hefty £1,200 a year by the time you reach the age of 54. A sum of ten times your gross income would not be excessive if you are buying at an early age when cover is cheap. Many term life assurance contracts allow you to increase the cover at various intervals to take account of inflation, but of course the premium will increase too.

Your current employer may provide life cover at three to four times the level of your income already. But bear in mind that your next employer may not, in which case you will have to buy it yourself, possibly when you are much older, when it will be more expensive.

If your employer provides life cover, it will probably pay to treat it as a bonus and buy your own life cover as well.

LIFE COVER

Term assurance and convertible term assurance

Term assurance and convertible term assurance are very similar; both pay a lump sum if you die within the agreed term of the policy. The object is to provide cash for your dependants during the time when they are not able to look after themselves. The term of the policy may be anything from, say, five to twenty-five years.

Typically, as a young woman, you would take out convertible term assurance for twenty-five years to cover the period when you are likely to have young children.

The difference between term cover and convertible term assurance is that you can, as the name implies, convert the convertible term policy into another type of life assurance.

You might, for example, want to switch to the more comprehensive whole life cover which will provide a lump sum for your spouse or dependants – whenever you die. Convertible term assurance gives you this option to switch without being obliged to give evidence of good health. Make sure the policy also includes options to increase the cover, otherwise you will only be able to convert it to whole life cover for the original sum assured.

The importance of buying convertible term as opposed to term assurance is that if you contract an illness at a later date, you may well find that premiums for whole life cover are high. In a worst possible situation where you develop, say, cancer, it will be impossible to obtain life assurance at any price.

Convertible term assurance ensures your ability to obtain life assurance at some time in the future, whatever your state of health at the time.

If you are currently single and with no dependants this may not seem very important, but it will be at a later date if you marry and have children.

It is important to bear in mind the effects of inflation on benefits. Either overinsure when you are very young and the premiums are cheap, or make sure you have the option to increase the benefits, preferably throughout the term of the policy.

You usually buy straight term assurance if you need to keep costs to an absolute minimum. Price is the most important factor you need to worry about and the cheapest policy will be the best. However, different companies have varying views on what lives they are prepared to insure. Some will insure you almost without question up to a certain limit – say £50,000. Others may quote a cheaper rate but will be very selective about the type of risk they insure. For example, they may insist on a full medical or load the premiums for anyone doing anything other than a totally safe job. It will pay to shop around or take independent advice, as there are wide variations in the cost. One company may charge more than double another for the same cover.

For example, convertible term assurance can cost £152 a year for £100,000 cover over 15 years for a 29-year-old woman. Another company, which is far from being the most expensive, can charge £356 for the same cover.

Generally, it is almost always better to pay a little more for the conversion right and for the right to increase the level of cover. But price is not the only criterion with convertible term cover. Make sure that the company from which you purchase your policy has other policies into which it is worth switching; the conversion option is useless if it hasn't. For example, you might want to convert your policy into whole life cover or a savings type policy. There is no point doing this if the company from which you bought your convertible term contract charges double the going rate for whole life cover, or has a dismal investment track record and its savings type policies are poor value for money.

You should also make sure that the policy has an option to regularly increase the sum assured. What may seem like sufficient life cover today can easily become totally inadequate after five years, particularly if inflation is high. A good policy gives you the option to increase the sum assured – without evidence of health – at various stages in the life of the policy. You will, of course, have to pay more when you increase the cover.

An increasing number of policies offer cover and premiums linked to changes in the Retail Prices Index. This ensures that the value of the cover keeps pace with inflation.

The table below shows monthly premiums for £100,000 worth of cover for varying periods and for women of different ages. The rates quoted are from a leading life assurance company, but they are not necessarily the cheapest.

Term assurance is most commonly used to provide cover while the children are young or to pay off a mortgage, should you die before the loan is repaid.

But it has other applications. You might need to cover your life for

Annual premium for £100,000, renewable convertible term cover

Female, Age Next Birthday	Term in Years					
	5	10	15	20	25	30
	£	£	£	£	£	£
20	132.75	132.75	139.65	159.55	204.05	252.35
25	132.75	132.75	139.65	159.55	204.05	252.35
30	132.75	132.75	144.25	184.15	231.65	293.75
35	139.65	154.60	194.85	281.10	368.15	462.80
40	194.85	245.45	339.75	493.85	626.10	777.90
45	324.80	460.50	626.10	863.00	1075.75	1298.85
50	627.25	860.70	1096.45	1485.15	1801.40	
55	1097.60	1441.45	1825.05	2443.10		
60	1711.70	2364.90	2996.25			

Source: *Scottish Equitable*

seven years after you have given away assets to provide cash for any potential Inheritance Tax liability. If you give things away but die within seven years, there may be an Inheritance Tax bill (see Chapter 1 for full details). After seven years, the liability disappears.

For example, say at age 65 you gave a grandson £200,000. The potential Inheritance Tax liability if you die within seven years of making the gift is between £24,000 and £4,800, depending on when you die. So you would use term assurance to cover you for the seven years when your estate has a potential Inheritance Tax liability.

Family income benefit
This is a variation on straight term cover. Instead of paying a lump sum when you die, it pays a monthly income until the end of the term. Most family income benefit policies are commuted for a lump sum because the tax treatment of the income is disadvantageous.

Whole life
This policy has no specific term and provides a lump sum when you die – whenever that might be. It is only essential if your partner or spouse or other dependants could not live comfortably on their income after you die.

You might, for example, have a disabled child needing expensive residential care if you were no longer able to provide it. Whole life cover would ensure that there would be a lump sum, payable on your death, which could be invested to produce an income to cover the cost of full-time care.

Where possible, people should try to make provision for their partner through savings and pensions policies and provided this is adequate, whole life cover may not be essential. Children can usually take care of themselves by the time you are likely to die, except for unusual circumstances such as handicap, where they are likely to remain dependent.

Whole life cover is more expensive than convertible term because as you will inevitably die, the policy is guaranteed to pay out at some stage. With convertible term cover, the policy pays out only if you die before the policy expires. At a young age, the likelihood of this happening is fairly remote, and can be calculated quite accurately by the insurance company's actuary. So convertible term, if you buy when young, is cheap.

Whole life cover is also used to provide for an unavoidable Inheritance Tax liability. For many people, their main asset is the house they live in. You cannot avoid Inheritance Tax by giving it away to, say, your children and continuing to live in the property. This is called a gift with reservation and the transfer does not avoid Inheritance Tax.

If, for example, the house is worth more than £140,000 – the 1991-92 starting point for Inheritance Tax – your children will have to pay Inheritance Tax at 40 per cent on the excess over £140,000 when you die and they inherit the property. This might mean that they have to sell the property in order to meet the tax bill.

A whole life policy to provide a cash sum sufficient to pay the liability when you die would solve this problem. Of course, this may not matter if the house is to be sold anyway and the proceeds split between several children or grandchildren.

Many people believe that whole life cover, in this context, is not necessary because a spouse is able to inherit the property free of Inheritance Tax. But if you put off obtaining life cover until there is only one partner left, the cost of obtaining the cover when you are, say, sixty or more, is very high.

For example, whole life cover of £100,000 costs around £800 a year

Cost of £50,000 whole life cover at varying ages

Female age	Annual Premium £	Monthly Premium £
20	382.00	33.00
25	384.50	33.00
30	424.50	37.00
35	494.50	43.00
40	597.00	51.50
45	739.50	63.50
50	944.50	82.00
55	1229.50	106.50
60	1637.00	141.50
65	2174.50	190.00

Source: Scottish Equitable

at age thirty. By the time you are sixty-five, the same cover will cost £4,800 to £5,200.

Joint life policies

Since most married couples have no idea who will die first and therefore who will have to pay the Inheritance Tax bill, or be left shouldering the responsibility for the mortgage, joint life policies are often used in this context. They come in two forms: 'joint life, first death' policies which pay out on the death of the first partner and are used for mortgage protection or any situation where the survivor will have difficulty managing financially, and 'joint life, second death' policies, which pay out on the death of the second partner and are used almost exclusively in Inheritance Tax planning, where the liability does not arise until the second partner dies. You should insure for sufficient to cover any potential inheritance tax liability.

Like all life assurance, the younger you are when you buy joint life cover, the cheaper it is. However, the younger you are, the greater the likelihood of divorce. Once divorced you will no longer want, or be able, to transfer the property to the spouse free of Inheritance Tax; nor will you want your former spouse or partner to benefit from the proceeds of a mortgage protection policy – so you will need single life cover.

As always, the later you buy life assurance, the more expensive it becomes. Although you may have saved premiums on the joint life cover, any gain will probably be cancelled out by the higher cost of paying for single life cover, should you divorce at a later date.

For this reason, generally speaking, if you are buying when young it is better to go for two separate policies (say convertible term) on your own lives, rather than opting for the joint life policy.

Mortgage protection

Mortgage protection insurance is just another version of term assurance. It pays out sufficient to repay your home loan, should you die before the end of the term of the loan when the mortgage becomes repayable.

When you buy a house on a straight repayment loan you will probably be offered a mortgage protection policy by the lender. Do not be bullied

Joint whole life cover, last survivor – cost of cover

(a) *Male aged 40 next birthday, female aged 35 next birthday*

Sum Assured	Annual Premium £	Monthly Premium £
£10,000	97.00	8.20
£15,000	139.50	11.80
£20,000	182.00	15.40
£30,000	267.00	22.60
£40,000	352.00	29.80
£50,000	437.00	37.00
£60,000	522.00	44.20
£70,000	607.00	51.40
£80,000	692.00	58.60
£90,000	777.00	65.80
£100,000	862.00	73.00

(b) *Male aged 70 next birthday, female aged 65 next birthday*

Sum Assured	Annual Premium £	Monthly Premium £
£10,000	362.00	31.40
£15,000	537.00	46.60
£20,000	712.00	61.80
£30,000	1062.00	92.20
£40,000	1412.00	122.60
£50,000	1762.00	153.00
£60,000	2112.00	183.40
£70,000	2462.00	213.80
£80,000	2812.00	244.20
£90,000	3162.00	274.60
£100,000	3512.00	305.00

Source: Scottish Equitable

into having it if you already have sufficient life cover.

For a single person with no dependents, mortgage protection is not necessary, although do bear in mind that it will be more expensive to buy if you marry and decide you need cover at a later date.

Mortgage protection cover is generally included in the cost of with profit endowment or pension-linked loans.

Those who already have convertible term cover of four times gross salary may not need mortgage protection cover. Don't let the lender persuade you into buying something you do not want.

If you do not have convertible term cover, you will do better to go and buy it when you buy the property, rather than take mortgage protection cover, which doesn't have the conversion option. The lender will be just as happy to arrange convertible term cover as mortgage protection.

If you have a repayment loan, the mortgage protection cover will usually be decreasing term assurance. This means that the lump sum payable if you should die before the mortgage is repaid will reflect the fact that you are gradually repaying the loan.

This type of mortgage protection should be cheaper than convertible term (although this is not always the case, because of the huge differences in the premium rates charged by varying life companies).

For other types of loan where you are paying interest only on the borrowing and have associated life and pensions policies which eventually pay off the loan, the mortgage protection cover is straight term insurance, because the whole of the loan is outstanding until the

Annual premiums for mortgage protection cover – decreasing term – term 25 years

	Female (Non-smoker) Age					
Sum Assured	20	25	30	35	40	45
	£	£	£	£	£	£
£15,000	24.22	24.22	24.22	31.21	45.17	69.62
£20,000	28.30	28.30	28.30	37.61	56.23	88.82
£25,000	32.37	32.37	32.37	44.01	67.29	108.03
£30,000	36.44	36.44	36.44	50.41	78.35	127.24
£40,000	44.59	44.59	44.59	63.22	100.46	165.65
£50,000	52.74	52.74	52.74	76.02	122.58	204.06
£60,000	60.89	60.89	60.89	88.82	144.70	242.47
£70,000	69.04	69.04	69.04	101.63	166.81	280.88
£80,000	77.18	77.18	77.18	114.43	188.93	319.30
£90,000	85.33	85.33	85.33	127.24	211.04	357.71
£100,000	93.48	93.48	93.48	140.04	233.16	396.12

Source: Norwich Union

129

end of the term. The sum assured is usually set at the amount of the loan and is part of the insurance package, along with your endowment or pension premiums. With pension-linked home loans, you will be entitled to tax relief on both the pension premiums and the associated mortgage protection premiums.

Here again, you may well be offered a joint life policy if you are buying the property with a relative, partner, or spouse. In this case the policy pays out on the death of the first partner, not the second, and is known as 'joint life, first death' cover.

Joint life mortgage protection provides a cash lump sum, enough that if either partner dies, the remaining person has sufficient money to pay off the mortgage. This is clearly important where the breadwinner dies first, leaving a dependent non-earning partner or spouse and possibly children.

'Joint life, first death' cover is not much more expensive than single life cover and is good value for money. But if you can afford it, given that one in three marriages end in divorce, separate policies may well be the better long-term option.

Hybrid policies

In recent years, the insurance industry has introduced hybrid policies, usually with names like 'Plan for Life', 'Lifestyle', or 'Passport for Life'. These are a combination of straight life cover and the savings-type with profits endowment or unit linked life policy.

The idea is that you decide how much life cover you need and the balance is put into the savings part of the contract. However, you will generally find that the insurer reserves the right to increase the premiums on the straight life cover at various stages throughout the contract, dipping into the savings part of the contract to pay for the higher premiums.

You therefore cannot be certain what it will actually cost you for life cover in the future. You will generally be better off avoiding them altogether and buying straight life cover with level premiums and saving elsewhere.

PERMANENT HEALTH INSURANCE

Most people worry about dying and insure for the consequences of this

Premiums for 'joint life, first death' cover – 25 year term

Male aged 30, female aged 25		
Sum Assured	Monthly Premium £	Annual Premium £
£5,000	–	–
£10,000	10.00	116.00
£15,000	14.50	168.00
£20,000	19.00	220.00
£30,000	28.00	324.00
£40,000	37.00	428.00
£50,000	46.00	532.00
£60,000	55.00	636.00
£70,000	64.00	740.00
£80,000	73.00	844.00
£90,000	82.00	948.00
£100,000	91.00	1052.00

Male aged 55, female aged 50		
Sum Assured	Monthly Premium £	Annual Premium £
£5,000	–	–
£10,000	33.20	382.00
£15,000	49.30	567.00
£20,000	65.40	752.00
£30,000	97.60	1122.00
£40,000	129.80	1492.00
£50,000	162.00	1862.00
£60,000	194.20	2232.00
£70,000	226.40	2602.00
£80,000	258.60	2972.00
£90,000	290.80	3342.00
£100,000	323.00	3712.00

Source: Scottish Equitable

happening. Few people realise that you are far more likely to have an accident or serious illness and be unable to work or get about, than you are to die before the age of 65.

Permanent Health Insurance (PHI) provides cover for just such an eventuality. It pays a monthly income, usually up to age 60 or 65, if you have an accident or serious illness and are unable to work.

This is one area where women really do suffer. Because the actuarial tables used by the life companies concerning the incidence of sickness amongst women are years out of date, women pay more for PHI cover – usually about 50 per cent more – than men.

The situation is improving as the number of working women buying the cover increases. This gives the life companies a broader statistical base on which they can review the incidence of claims. But women are still penalized.

Cover for non-working women is available but is more difficult to obtain and there is usually a fairly low maximum benefit of around £7,500 a year. The insurers take the view that there is every incentive for a woman who is not employed, to remain 'ill' for as long as possible if she is being paid a monthly income for lying in bed.

Almost all women need this cover; clearly those earning and with dependent children or other relatives, and particularly the self-employed, need it the most.

Permanent health insurance varies widely in the terms and conditions of the policies available and this is one area where it will definitely pay to take independent financial advice, not least of all because it is not cheap.

There are many factors which will affect both the level of premiums and the conditions under which the benefits are paid. The insurance companies which offer this cover can be very tough about accepting you as a risk, because once you have taken out the policy, it cannot be cancelled by the company (although you can cancel it by discontinuing the premiums). No matter how many claims you make – even if you are unable to work for the rest of your life – the company has to pay until the benefit period expires.

Not surprisingly, PHI is one area of life assurance where there is considerable scope for dispute and litigation. With straight life cover you are either dead or you are not.

Some insurers are dealing with the difficulty by offering Dread Disease or Critical Illness PHI cover. This is better than nothing and is generally cheaper than full PHI cover, but it is not really very satisfactory because it limits the illnesses or disabling accidents for which a claim can be made.

If you are unable to work for the rest of your life, the sickness which has disabled you is immaterial. Critical Illness cover is the life companies' way of trying to play on people's fears of contracting cancer or having a heart attack whilst keeping premiums at a level which makes the cover easier to sell. Full PHI cover is far superior but is usually more expensive.

PHI gives you cover until the benefits under the policy expire. Given the fact that not everyone is desperately keen to work for the rest of their life, and taking into account the general incidence of malingering at work, it is not surprising that the life companies have to be very careful about whom they accept for PHI. They will usually expect you to have a medical before accepting you, and if you have had any serious illness, you may have the premiums heavily loaded to reflect the likelihood of your being ill and unable to work. There is frequently an exclusion for pre-existing conditions. In a worst possible case you may not be able to obtain cover at all.

Self-employed and non-employed women

Like non-employed housewives or househusbands, the self-employed are treated as second class citizens when it comes to PHI.

The insurance companies take the view that for these categories there are too many incentives to stay ill. And they do have a point. No-one is going to be in much of a hurry to be signed off by the doctor and returned to work if business is bad. Premiums will be loaded to reflect this fact. Depending on the job you do, the maximum cover obtainable may be relatively low.

The difficulty is that few people need PHI cover more than the self-employed whose income, very often, ceases the moment they stop work.

Some companies do not offer PHI for the self-employed or non-earning housewives or househusbands at all.

Deferral period

The aim of PHI is to provide income for a disaster, when you are seriously ill or disabled and may never work again or are unable even to run the household. It is not intended to supplement your income every time you take a week off for an attack of flu.

By accepting a deferral period, during which time payment of benefit is postponed, you can obtain substantial reductions in the premiums.

The length of deferral you decide to take will probably depend on the length of time your employer will pay your salary if you take sick leave.

For the self-employed, it will depend on how long you can keep your head above water financially before the benefits come into force. If you have a family, a large mortgage and little or no savings, this may not be much more than a month, or three months at the outside.

Where the breadwinner is employed, most families or single women can manage – albeit with the help of friends or relatives – if they are sick for, say, a month or so.

Employees in white-collar jobs may have their salary paid for anything up to six months. After that period, if you are disabled or seriously ill, you will probably find that your employer ceases to pay you, or pensions you off.

On the other hand, a factory worker may be paid for only a month if unable to work through sickness or accident. The length of deferral you are prepared to accept will therefore differ according to your personal circumstances.

– *For how much can I insure?*

Maximum cover is usually between two-thirds and three-quarters of your earnings at the time you become disabled or seriously ill. The reason for this is that the insurer wants to provide you with an incentive to get well and return to work. The idea is that you should not be better off financially when you are sick than earning.

This limit also takes into account that the benefits from a PHI policy are not taxable until they have been paid for a full fiscal year. So if you are permanently disabled, say, on 10 April 1991, the PHI benefits will not be taxable until 6 April 1993 – almost two years later.

Add to this the fact that you would also be entitled to tax-free State sickness benefit and it isn't difficult to understand why the insurance companies impose a maximum benefit which is less than your pre-claim earnings. Different policies have different definitions of income and some, for example, do not take into account bonuses – even although they may be regular and predictable. Some companies' definition may be gross earnings, others look at your take-home pay.

Most life companies also have a maximum benefit for which they will provide cover. This can be anything between £5,000 and £50,000 a year. A few companies have no maximum.

When deciding on the level of cover, you should take into account State benefits.

– *Does the job I do affect premiums?*

Yes. Premiums vary widely – not just between companies offering similar cover, but according to your occupation. Factory workers, for example, are much more likely to suffer an injury at work and premiums are therefore loaded to reflect this fact. Insurance company employees who lead a relatively quiet life – at least in the office – are deemed to be a good risk and cover is cheaper.

– *When can I claim?*

Clearly, you cannot claim until any deferral period has expired. Equally, if you are lying in bed in hospital with a broken back, fractured

State sickness and disability payments

Invalidity Pension, 1991-92	*£ per week*
Single person	52.00
Married couple	83.25
Invalidity allowance*	
Under 40	11.10
40-49	6.90
50-55 (female)	3.45
50-60 (male)	3.45
Short term sickness	
Single person	39.60
Married couple	64.10

Benefits are not taxable. All benefits are payable after 28 weeks, except short term sickness benefit, which is payable during the first 28 weeks.

* *Age when first falling ill.*

skull and unable to speak, no insurance company is going to dispute your claim. It is when you start to get better that the problems arise.

Once you make a claim, the definition of 'disability' and the level of benefits paid will vary from company to company.

If you are permanently unable to follow your normal occupation, you will receive benefits – but it may not be the full amount for which you have insured. Where you do not fully recover, you may still be able to do work of some kind, and many life offices take this into account and reduce benefits pro rata.

A few companies will pay benefit even if you do get another job – albeit not your previous job and at a lower salary. More often, benefit is reduced to take account of the fact that you may be able to get a suitable job which is not so well-paid.

Other companies reduce your benefit by the amount of actual income you are earning once you return to work. This in itself can provide a disincentive to get better. Some companies may review each case individually. Most will ask for medical reports if the disability looks like being permanent and having a serious effect on your earning capacity and ability to work. The majority of companies offer a waiver of premiums while you are claiming benefit.

Cost of permanent health insurance benefit, £100 a week, payable to woman age 60*

Age Next Birthday	Deferment Period		
	4 weeks	13 weeks	26 weeks
20	125.16	62.29	47.77
25	140.58	74.52	54.86
30	161.16	91.21	67.78
35	188.59	103.44	77.72
40	221.17	118.64	87.78
45	258.89	144.59	104.92
50	320.61	191.79	144.93
55	414.90	266.54	207.79

* *Clerical worker, premiums at ordinary rates.*
Source: Norwich Union

Conclusion

It isn't difficult to see that PHI can be a minefield and it is very important to take independent financial advice before signing up.

ACCIDENT AND DISABILITY INSURANCE

Accident and Disability insurance pays a lump sum if you are injured in an accident or permanently disabled. It pays no benefit if you are simply sick. Pure accident insurance would pay nothing if, for example, you suffered a stroke and were bedridden for the rest of your life. Accident and disability insurance may pay in these circumstances but the definition of 'permanently disabled' can be very specific.

Unlike permanent health insurance, accident and disability insurance is an annual contract; every year it has to be renewed, and insurers have a nasty way of upping the premiums if you have made a claim in the meantime.

It is of limited use in any case, since you have to lose a limb – an eye, a foot or hand – or be permanently disabled by an accident (sometimes, a disabling illness) before any benefits are paid. It is not worth bothering with accident and disability insurance if you have permanent health insurance. You will also find that the premiums are loaded if you play sports, particularly potentially dangerous activities like skiing or bicycle racing.

MEDICAL FEES INSURANCE

Strictly speaking, this is not life assurance. Medical fees insurance provides a sum of money to help pay for the cost of private medical treatment, should you fall ill and need in-patient hospital treatment. The advantage of this is that you avoid National Health waiting lists which can run to months – or years for some of the more common treatments.

Most medical fees insurance is paid for in full or in part by employers. You can obtain very large discounts if you are a member of a club or affinity group, such as the Civil Service.

However, medical fees insurance is not cheap, even with discounts, and in many instances it is not fully comprehensive. A few policies cover outpatient specialist treatment and orthodontic work – sometimes at an extra premium.

The lower costs 'budget plans' provide cover up to certain limits for hospital accommodation, surgeon's or physician's fees, nursing and treatment costs.

Probably the best and most affordable type of contract is the plan pioneered by Private Patients Plan (PPP) and now copied by British United Provident Association (BUPA). This pays fees for private medical care in the event that the waiting list for treatment under the National Health Service is six weeks or longer. It is very much cheaper than the full medical fees cover.

Medical fees insurance is an annual contract and the premium is likely to go up every year, especially if you have a series of expensive claims. The insurers can also refuse to renew the cover. It is virtually impossible to obtain over the age of 60 unless you have previously been insured with a company.

There are also major exclusions such as anything to do with childbirth unless it is a complication, drug- and alcohol-induced illnesses and pre-existing conditions. For example, if you have had kidney trouble, the policy will not pay out if there is a recurrence of the complaint and you need hospital treatment.

Most people who have medical fees insurance receive it as a perk from an employer – either free or at a subsidized rate. If you have to pay for it yourself it is expensive.

Given that few private hospitals have surgeons and physicians working round the clock, in an emergency you are probably better off being treated under the NHS, particularly for something like a brain haemorrhage or heart attack. Minor operations such as hernia or varicose veins are usually not expensive to pay for outright.

The cost of medical fees insurance can vary from company to company and from year to year. Like car insurance or household insurance, you will need to shop around for insurance every year.

Premiums vary widely depending on the level of cover you require, where you live and your age and medical track record, and you will need to take independent advice in order to obtain the best deal if you are paying for this cover yourself. If your employer, club or affinity group runs a scheme you will have no choice in terms of the insurer used – only the amount of cover.

TAX

The benefits paid out under most straight life assurance contracts are free of income and capital gains tax and are known as 'qualifying' life policies.

Single women, divorcees, widows and single parents should make sure that life policies are written in trust to avoid the proceeds being included in their estate and subject to Inheritance Tax.

This will also apply in certain circumstances for married women, where the proceeds are intended for someone other than your spouse. Remember, although the proceeds of a life policy are usually tax free, the investment income generated when the proceeds are invested are taxable in the usual way.

The benefits payable under some savings type contracts and guaranteed income bonds where the life assurance cover is small and which are designed to run for less than ten years may be taxable in certain circumstances. These are known as non-qualifying policies. Check on the tax position before you buy. This is generally only a problem for higher rate taxpayers.

Life policies taken out before March 1984 are eligible for tax relief on premiums. For this reason they are generally worth maintaining. Life premiums paid under a personal pension policy also qualify for tax relief at the personal pension rate. (See Chapter 3 on Pensions for more details.)

Savings type life policies

These should not really be regarded as life assurance policies, since the amount of cover is minimal. The most common are with profit endowments and unit linked life policies. All savings type policies are dealt with in Chapter 2 which covers savings and investments.

Medical limits

Provided you are in good health, you should have no difficulty obtaining life assurance cover. All life companies will ask you for details of any serious illnesses when you fill in the application form.

The insurance company will generally insure almost anyone who claims to be in good health without insisting upon a medical examination, but only up to a certain limit, usually around £50,000;

this figure can vary from company to company. Above this limit, the company will want you to have a medical and may ask for one in any case if you have had a serious illness.

Life cover may be difficult to obtain if you have suffered from nervous complaints such as severe depression; the life company may impose a suicide exclusion.

Always declare any serious illnesses on the application form. If you don't, the life company may refuse to pay the benefits to your dependants on the grounds of non-disclosure.

Many companies offer discounts for non-smokers, but the best premium from a life company that does not offer discounts may still be cheaper than another company offering discounts.

$\mathcal{G}$ETTING HELP

There is no use pretending that managing your financial affairs will necessarily be simple. Life assurance, pensions, savings and investments are complex areas which tax the minds of experts as well as the uninitiated. You will undoubtedly need help and advice.

Throughout this book, the recommendation has been to seek the help of an independent financial adviser (IFA), and it is important to understand the changes that have come about in the way financial products are sold as a result of new legislation.

In 1986 the Financial Services Act came into being and parts of it are still being implemented. Its aim is to protect the buyer of financial products and services from cowboy financial advisers, and it has many important implications for the consumer.

First, there is now an industry-wide fund which will pay compensation to investors who suffer losses when firms of intermediaries fail.

Maximum compensation is, however, low – 100 per cent of the first £30,000 and 90 per cent of the next £20,000, making a maximum of £48,000. The situation is under review by the Securities and Investment Board (SIB), the industry watchdog, but the upshot is likely to be a cutting back of the areas where compensation can be claimed – not an improvement.

Equally important, the Financial Services Act introduced the concept of 'polarization'. Everyone who sells financial products or services must clearly identify themselves as being either a truly impartial, independent financial adviser, able to choose a suitable product from the whole range on offer, or the tied salesman or appointed representative of just one financial institution, able to sell only that company's products.

The implications of this are obvious. No one company produces the best product in all areas – life assurance, pensions, savings, or permanent health. One company may have a top performing pension fund, but no permanent health contract at all. In addition, there are dozens of insurance companies, fund managers and the like who sell products which are very poor value for money.

To get the best product in every area of your finances, you must consult an independent financial adviser. But the situation is confusing, and indeed is likely to become more so. The major high street banks and building societies, with the notable exception of National Westminster and Bradford & Bingley, have all opted to be 'tied' to a financial institution. For example, Halifax is tied to Standard Life and Nationwide to Guardian Royal Exchange.

The high street banks – except National Westminster – are all tied to their own in-house insurance companies, so Barclays Bank is tied to Barclays Life and can sell only Barclays Life's products.

However, the legislation as it stands allows them to run an IFA subsidiary and you will find that if you turn down a recommendation from a bank salesperson on the grounds that it is not impartial, the chances are the bank manager or salesperson will then refer you to their independent arm.

To make matters even more confusing, this is all likely to change again as soon as we move into a Europewide financial services market in 1992, because Europe does not have polarization.

The third important plank of consumer protection introduced in the Financial Services Act is regulation. Anyone who sells financial products or services must be registered with one of the Self Regulatory Organisations (SROs) that police the various financial markets.

The four SROs are the Securities and Futures Authority, which monitors the activities of stockbrokers, futures and commodity brokers and dealers; the Investment Managers Regulatory Organisation (IMRO), to which all the fund management companies and some of the larger firms of IFAs belong; the Life Assurance and Unit Trust Regulatory Organisation (LAUTRO), which controls the activities of the direct salesmen and appointed representatives which work for the life assurance companies and unit trust groups; and the Financial Intermediaries, Managers and Brokers Regulatory Association (FIMBRA), to which most of the smaller firms of independent financial advisers belong.

In addition there are professional organizations, such as accountants and solicitors, whose members are allowed to give financial advice as Recognised Professional Bodies (RPBs). These include the accountants' associations such as the Institute of Chartered Accountants of England and Wales, (also the Scottish and Northern Ireland organizations, as well as the certified accountants), the Law Society, which covers all solicitors (and the Scottish and Northern Ireland counterparts), The Institute of Actuaries and the Insurance Brokers Registration Council.

How to find an independent financial adviser

Finding a competent and reliable IFA, if you don't have one already, is rather easier said than done.

While the majority are honest and hardworking, there is no doubt that there are still some incompetent and unprofessional advisers around. Hopefully, there are not too many crooks and cowboys left.

IFAs are not yet obliged to have any professional qualifications, although they do need to have had some relevant experience. However, the best firms will have qualified tax experts, lawyers, insurance consultants, investment managers and mortgage brokers on the staff and will be able to offer a wide range of services – anything from setting up a trust or managing a portfolio of £500,000 to finding a low start mortgage and arranging life assurance.

All independent advisers have to belong to one of the Self Regulatory Organisations (SROs). Most belong to FIMBRA, the Financial Intermediaries, Managers and Brokers Regulatory Association. Some of the larger firms of independent advisers are members of IMRO, the Investment Management Regulatory Organisation. And of course, many stockbrokers offer not just investment services but a wide range of financial advice on everything from life assurance and pensions to mortgages.

IFA firms range from literally one man and a telephone to large concerns with hundreds of consultants. Their level of expertise varies enormously. Some are only authorized to sell life assurance, pensions and unit trust products, while others can give advice on anything from taxation to trusts or investment management to self-administered pension schemes for small businesses.

Personal recommendation can be useful, provided the person making the recommendation is qualified to judge the quality of the service they are receiving. A friend might suggest you go to a particular adviser because he or she is friendly and efficient in processing your business. But be careful and ensure that the adviser will be able to fulfil your needs.

IFA Promotions, which represents IFAs, will give you the name, address and telephone number of six IFAs in your area.

Most banks and building societies are tied to one particular life company although many also offer an independent financial advisory service and many firms of accountants run their own independent financial advisory services alongside the tax department.

Some IFAs have moved towards fee-charging rather than taking their remuneration in the form of commission. The magazine *Money Management*, which specializes in this market, runs a register of fee-charging intermediaries and if you write or telephone, will supply you with details of fee-charging IFAs in your area. But remember, this does not in itself guarantee any better level of service.

If investment advice figures high on your list of priorities, then it could be worth considering one of the firms of private client stockbrokers who also have a fully-fledged personal financial planning department.

Life assurance and pensions might be your requirement, in which case the British Insurance and Investment Brokers Association of the Insurance Brokers Registration Council and the Society of Pension Consultants all require their members to be properly qualified and will supply you with the names of member firms in your area. The Appendix at the end of this book lists the names and addresses of various useful organizations.

How to complain

Hopefully, your financial affairs will run smoothly. But things do go wrong. It is well known that the administration of many major life offices is less efficient than it ought to be. Banks and credit card companies have suffered criticism of their administration and charges, and it is inevitable that there will be problems from time to time.

But if things do go wrong, it helps if you know the various routes to settling your complaint.

All financial institutions and advisers are supposed to inform their customers of the complaints procedures and the areas of complaint which can be dealt with, but not all do.

One major exclusion from all complaints procedures is that you cannot complain about investment performance just because it is poor. You can only object in this context if you were sold, say, an equity-linked investment where the value can fluctuate, and you had not been told that you might lose money. This would be considered negligence, rather than a complaint about the investment performance.

The general rule when complaining applies, whoever you are dealing with. Take up the matter first with the individual or institution concerned, if necessary writing to the chief executive if you get no satisfaction from junior members of staff.

If this fails, there are several courses of action open to you. You can ask to have your complaint referred to the relevant Ombudsman. This is a free service and the terms are broadly similar.

The Ombudsman, of which there are five – Insurance, Banking, Pensions, Building Societies and the Investment Referee – will investigate your complaint and make a decision. They have powers to make awards up to £100,000.

In the case of the Insurance, Banking and Pensions Ombudsmen, the Ombudsman's decision is binding on the institution but you, the complainant, are free to pursue the matter in court if you don't like the decision.

The Investment Referee's decisions are binding on both parties and if you agree to allow him to adjudicate, you will lose the right to go to court. In the case of the Building Societies Ombudsman the decision is binding on neither party, although if the Ombudsman finds against a building society and the society rejects his decision, the reason must be publicized.

If the complaint is about an independent financial adviser then you should write first to the firm in question. If you are not satisfied, you should then write to the IFA's watchdog organisation, the SRO, which will be on the firm's writing paper.

Most IFAs will be members of either FIMBRA, IMRO or the SFA.

Some may be members of more than one SRO.

The SRO should investigate your complaint and has powers to discipline its members if they have broken the rules. Where there has been a clear breach, the SRO will generally press its member to settle with the client.

You can also ask to have your complaint referred to FIMBRA's Consumer Arbitration Scheme which operates like the Ombudsman.

If your complaint is against a stockbroker, you can ask to have the matter referred to the Stock Exchange Complaints Bureau.

Complaining to the relevant SRO is an alternative to having the matter referred to the Ombudsman – or of course, you can complain to both.

If you are not happy that the SRO has properly investigated your complaint then you can ask to have the matter referred to SIB, the overall industry watchdog which polices the SROs.

Compensation

If you have lost money as a result of the negligence, incompetence or collapse of a business, compensation is available in some instances.

– *The Financial Services Act Compensation Scheme*

This will provide compensation of up to £48,000 – 100 per cent of the first £30,000, 90 per cent of the next £20,000 – in the event of an independent financial adviser, investment manager or stockbroker failing. The Stock Exchange also provides compensation on top of this up to £500,000 per claim (a good reason for using a firm of private client stockbrokers to handle your investments).

However, the scheme does not cover the activities of direct salesmen, appointed representatives or tied agents of life companies or unit trust groups. If an appointed representative of a life company, for example, misappropriates your money, your only course of action is to complain to the company concerned.

This is a very fraught area. There have been cases where the insurance company has refused to pay up on the grounds that where an appointed representative was putting the clients' money into his own bank account rather than into an investment with the life company concerned, this constituted unauthorized deposit taking and was therefore outside the Financial Services Act. But it has been pointed out many times that *all* misappropriation is outside the Financial Services Act.

- The Policyholders' Protection Act

The 1976 Policyholders' Protection Act provides compensation of up to 90 per cent of the sum invested, without limit, if a UK insurance company fails. The only exception is where the promised benefits are 'excessive', in which case the compensation may be scaled down. You will not be covered if you invest with a non-UK insurance company – as investors in Gibraltar-based Signal Life know to their cost.

- The 1979 Banking Act – compensation

This provides compensation for investors of 75 per cent of the first £20,000 deposited – a maximum of £15,000 – in the event that a UK-based bank fails. If you are of an anxious disposition, keep your money in one of the big name, high street banks.

- The Building Societies' Compensation Scheme

This provides compensation of 90 per cent of the first £20,000 invested – a maximum of £18,000 – in the event that a building society fails. Go for one of the top ten if you are the worrying kind.

- The Insurance Brokers' Registration Council Compensation Scheme

This covers investors who have lost money with a Registered Insurance Brokers through the collapse of the firm, or the broker's negligence or incompetence. However, before it comes into play, all other forms of compensation have to be explored. This usually involves sueing the broker for damages and waiting to see if the broker's professional indemnity insurance pays out – not something which most people can afford to do if they have already lost money. The IBRC scheme has paid out very little as a result.

*U*SEFUL ADDRESSES

REGULATORY BODIES

The Securities and Investment Board (SIB) (overall investment and
   financial services watchdog)
Gavrelle House
2-14 Bunhill Row
London EC1Y 8RA
Tel: (071) 638 1240

THE SELF REGULATORY ORGANISATIONS (SROs)

Financial Intermediaries, Managers and Brokers Regulatory
   Association (FIMBRA)
Hertsmere House
Hertsmere Road
London E14 4AB
Tel: (071) 538 8860

Investment Management Regulatory Organisation (IMRO)
Broadwalk House
5 Appold Street
London EC2A 2LL
Tel: (071) 628 6022

Life Assurance and Unit Trust Regulatory Organisation (LAUTRO)
3rd Floor
103 New Oxford Street
London WC1A 1PT
Tel: (071) 379 0444

The Securities and Futures Authority (SFA)
The Stock Exchange Tower
Old Broad Street
London EC2N 1HP
Tel: (071) 256 9000

RECOGNIZED PROFESSIONAL BODIES

The Chartered Association of Certified Accountants
29 Lincoln's Inn Fields
London WC2A 3EE
Tel: (071) 242 6855

The Institute of Actuaries
Staple Inn Hall
High Holborn
London WC1V 7QJ
Tel: (071) 242 0106

The Institute of Chartered Accountants of Ireland
Chartered Accountants House
87-89 Pembroke Road
Dublin 4
Eire
Tel: (0001) 680400

The Institute of Chartered Accountants of England & Wales
P.O. Box 433
Chartered Accountants' Hall
Moorgate Place
London EC2P 2BJ
Tel: (071) 628 7060

The Institute of Chartered Accountants of Scotland
27 Queen Street
Edinburgh EH2 1LA
Tel: (031) 225 5673

Insurance Brokers Registration Council
15 St. Helen's Place
London EC3A 6DS
Tel: (071) 588 4387

The Law Society of England and Wales
113 Chancery Lane
London WC2A 1PL
Tel: (071) 242 1222

The Law Society of Northern Ireland
Law Society House
90-106 Victoria Street
Belfast BT1 3JZ
Tel: (0232) 231614

The Law Society of Scotland
26 Drumsheugh Gardens
Edinburgh EH3 7YR
Tel: (031) 226 7411

BANKS

The Bank of England (overall banking supervisor)
Threadneedle Street
London EC2R 8AH
Tel: (071) 601 4444

British Bankers Association (BBA) (trade association)
10 Lombard Street
London EC3V 9EL
Tel: (071) 623 4001

BUILDING SOCIETIES AND OTHER LENDERS

Association of Mortgage Lenders
c/o London & Manchester Assurance
Winslade Park
Exeter EX5 1DS
Tel: (0392) 282140

The Building Societies Association and Council of Mortgage
Lenders (trade association)
3 Savile Row
London W1X 1AF
Tel: (071) 437 0655

Building Societies Registry and Commission (overall supervisor of
building societies)
15-17 Great Marlborough Street
London W1V 2AX
Tel: (071) 437 9992

FINANCE HOUSES

Finance Houses Association (trade association)
18 Upper Grosvenor Street
London W1X 9PB
Tel: (071) 491 2783

INSURANCE COMPANIES

The Association of British Insurers (trade association)
Aldermary House
10-15 Queen Street
London EC4N 1TT
Tel: (071) 248 4477

Associated Scottish Life Offices (trade association)
23 St. Andrews Square
Edinburgh EH2 1AQ
Tel: (031) 556 7171

The Department of Trade and Industry (overall supervisor)
1-19 Victoria Street
London SW1H 0ET
Tel: (071) 215 5000

Linked Life Assurance Group (trade association)
6th Floor East
Lansdowne House
Berkeley Square
London W1X 5DH
Tel: (071) 409 0287

UNIT TRUSTS

The Unit Trust Association (trade association)
65 Kingsway
London WC2B 6TD
Tel: (071) 831 0898

INVESTMENT TRUSTS

The Association of Investment Trust Companies (trade association)
Park House
6th Floor
16 Finsbury Circus
London EC2M 7JJ
Tel: (071) 588 5347

BROKERS

The Association of Private Client Investment Managers and
    Stockbrokers (APCIMS)
20 Dysart Street
London EC2A 2BX
Tel: (071) 410 6868

The British Insurance and Investment Brokers Association
Biba House
14 Bevis Marks
London EC3A 7NT
Tel: (071) 623 9043

The International Stock Exchange (trade association)
The Stock Exchange
London EC2N 1HP
Tel: (071) 588 2355

Money Management Register of Fee Based IFAs
Greystoke Place
Fetter Lane
London EC4A 1ND
Tel: (071) 405 6969

PENSIONS

The Association of Consulting Actuaries
P.O. Box 144
Norfolk House
Wellesley Road
Croydon, Surrey
CR9 3EB
Tel: (081) 668 8040

Joint Office of the Superannuation Funds Office and Occupational
    Pensions Board (overall supervisor of pensions)
Lynwood Road
Thames Ditton
Surrey
KT20 0DP
Tel: (081) 398 4242

The National Association of Pension Funds (trade association for
    occupational pension funds)
12-18 Grosvenor Gardens
London SW1W 0DH
Tel: (071) 730 0585

The Occupational Pensions Advisory Service
11 Belgrave Road
London SW1V 1RB
Tel: (071) 233 8080

The Society of Pension Consultants
Ludgate House
Ludgate Circus
London EC4A 2AB
Tel: (071) 353 1688

OMBUDSMEN

The Banking Ombudsman
Citadel House
5-11 Fetter Lane
London EC4A 1BR
Tel: (071) 583 1395

The Building Societies Ombudsman
35-37 Grosvenor Gardens
London SW1X 7AW
Tel: (071) 931 0044

The Insurance Ombudsman
31 Southampton Row
London WC1B 5JH
Tel: (071) 242 8613

The Investment Referee
6 Frederick's Place
London EC2R 8BT
Tel: (071) 796 3065

The Parliamentary Ombudsman (must be referred through an MP
  – deals with maladministration by government departments,
  including the Inland Revenue)
Church House
Great Smith Street
London SW1P 3BW
Tel: (071) 276 2130

The Pensions Ombudsman
11 Belgrave Road
London SW1V 1RB
Tel: (071) 834 9144

OTHERS

Chase de Vere Investments (produce an impartial guide to all PEP
  schemes on offer)
63 Lincoln's Inn Fields
London WC2A 3JU
Tel: (071) 404 5766

Department for National Savings
Charles House
375 Kensington High Street
London W14 8SD
Tel: (071) 605 9300

Freeline Social Security (Benefit Agency: offers free advice on
  Social Security entitlements, pensions, National Insurance, etc)
Tel: (0800) 666555

IFA Promotions (will provide names and addresses of independent
  financial advisers)
4th Floor
28 Greville Street
London EC1N 8SU
Helpline—Tel: (071) 200 3000

The National Council for One Parent Families
255 Kentish Town Road
London NW5 2LX
Tel: (071) 267 1361

The National House Building Council
58 Portland Place
London W1N 4BU
Tel: (071) 637 1248

The Office of Fair Trading (licences credit brokers)
15-25 Field House
Breams Buildings
London EC4A 1PR
Tel: (071) 242 2858

Royal Institution of Chartered Surveyors
12 Great George Street
London SW1P 3AD
Tel: (071) 222 7000

The *Which* Bookshop (part of The Consumers Association)
359-361 Euston Road
London NW1 3AL
Tel: (071) 486 5544

INDEX